The INSANITY of UNBELIEF

The INSANITY of UNBELIEF

A Journalist's Journey from
BELIEF *to* SKEPTICISM *to* DEEP FAITH

How Science and the Supernatural
Changed My Life

MAX DAVIS

DESTINY IMAGE₀ PUBLISHERS, INC.
P.O. Box 310, Shippensburg, PA 17257-0310
"Promoting Inspired Lives."

This book and all other Destiny Image, Revival Press, MercyPlace, Fresh Bread, Destiny Image Fiction, and Treasure House books are available at Christian bookstores and distributors worldwide.

For a U.S. bookstore nearest you, call 1-800-722-6774.
For more information on foreign distributors, call 717-532-3040.
Reach us on the Internet: www.destinyimage.com.

ISBN 13 TP: 978-0-7684-4149-9
ISBN 13 Ebook: 978-0-7684-8811-1

For Worldwide Distribution, Printed in the U.S.A.
5 6 7 8 / 16 15

ACKNOWLEDGMENTS

I would like to express my appreciation to *Nick Kalavota* for taking time to interview with me concerning biblical archeology; to *Sharon "Katie" Fellner* for her medical expertise and reviewing the medical records; and to *Acie and Marolyn Ford, David and Sheila Yaniv, Bruce Van Natta, Bruce Carlson, Bob Bell,* and *Malcolm Richard* for taking time to share their inspiring stories with me. Thanks to *Karen Hardin,* my super-agent, for believing in me. I believe in you, too! Thanks to *John Manda* for his timely "words" that kept me going so many days; to *Fred* and *Lydia Fellner* for their ongoing support; and to *Larry Koenig, Carter Featherston, Chris Rust, Ron Checki,* and *Ron DiCianni* for being good friends, always reading my stuff, and encouraging me to stay the course. Thanks to *Richard Exley* for helping me through my dark night of the soul. You will always be my pastor of writing. Thank you, also, to *Kyle Loffelmacher* and *Ronda Ranalli* at Destiny Image for digging the book. And finally, thank you *Alanna* for always holding my hands up, being an incredible writing partner, and going the distance with me. I love you, babe!

ENDORSEMENTS

In *The Insanity of Unbelief,* Max points the way to truth in one of the clearest declarations I have yet to read on the subject. With tender and convincing passion, Max grabs the readers by the hands and leads them to truth and freedom.

Ron DiCianni
Renowned Christian artist and bestselling author
Winner of six Gold Medallion awards for Christian publishing

Let me cut to the chase. I am a committed Christian. I have even had a close, personal, real-life encounter with Jesus. But I still have times when my faith is in shambles, times when I think, *If God exists, it doesn't matter because He clearly is not involved in my life in any way whatsoever.* I hate those times! Thank God for Max Davis and his book *The Insanity of Unbelief.* This book is so engaging and so refreshing. It addresses the issue of unbelief head on, makes you feel normal for having your doubts, and then squarely plants the evidence that God is real and does care about you and me and does indeed answer prayers, sometimes through incredible miracles. You will never be the same after reading this book! It is a powerful, powerful, powerful book!

Larry J. Koenig, PhD
Bestselling author of *Mental Toughness* and *Smart Discipline*

Poignant yet scholarly, provocative yet kindhearted, Max Davis has written a book that shows how truly sane it is to believe though living in a culture of unbelief. It's a book that will empower your faith and one you can feel good about giving to your friends.

Carter Featherston
Founder, RestoreOne Ministry
Graduate of Dallas Theological Seminary

The Insanity of Unbelief is one of the most important books I have ever read. If I could, I would stand on the street corner and hand out copies to everyone I meet. I don't think I'm going too far when I suggest that it's going to become a classic.

Richard Exley
Bestselling author and radio personality
Pastor, Gateway Church, Shreveport, Louisiana

To
A
World
That
Needs
Desperately
To
Believe

CONTENTS

Chapter 1

AN UNLIKELY SKEPTIC

A faith without some doubts is like a human body without any antibodies in it. People who blithely go through life too busy or indifferent to ask hard questions about why they believe as they do will find themselves defenseless against either the experience of tragedy or the probing questions of a smart skeptic. —Timothy Keller, The Reason for God[1]

One day back in the early 1980s, while studying Journalism at the University of Mississippi, I was asked by one of my professors if I would please stand. The class was a smaller one, seventy-five or perhaps one hundred students, and I was curious as to why he would make such a request when to my knowledge he had never before asked anyone else to stand. But because I had a solid grade and had turned in all of my assignments, I didn't feel particularly threatened and readily obeyed.

Once I was on my feet, the professor proceeded to ask me if it was true, as he had heard, that I was a Bible believing Christian. Apparently the word was out. And it was true. I was a committed Christ-follower, and because I was also a scholarship athlete, I had greater visibility than others. All of this had nothing to do with the class subject, but evidently this professor thought my faith was an issue that needed addressing.

When I answered "yes" to his question, his polite, upbeat attitude instantly turned rude and arrogant. In front of my peers, he began to insult my intelligence, belittle my faith, and discredit the Bible. To him there was absolutely no doubt that science and academia had shown the pure *insanity of such belief.* To accept the God of the Bible as true meant leaving common sense behind and taking an erroneous leap of faith into a deep abyss of irrationality. What about all the suffering and injustices in the world? How could God allow such things to persist? Science has proven evolution. What about the untold atrocities that have happened throughout history in the name of religion? On and on he went. To him, Christians were simple, narrow-minded, gullible, and it was people like us who had hindered the growth of humankind.

As a young college student, I stood there intimidated by this man's perceived intelligence and his perceived authority on the matters of which he spoke. At a total loss for any convincing words, I was unable to give a sound, rational rebuttal to his onslaughts. I think I mumbled something to the tune of, "Uh…'cause the Bible says so," which only seemed to further fuel his case. The bottom line was that this professor had ripped me, leaving me humiliated, embarrassed, and questioning my faith. Despite a few snickers, there were students present whom I knew were also believers, and they felt ripped as well.

I walked away that day limping spiritually, clinging desperately to what little shred of faith I had left. Looking back, I can only say what sustained me during that period of my life was a firm foundation in God's Word, fellowship with other believers, and an out-of-the-box supernatural incident I had experienced a few months earlier. A group of us clung together during our time at the university, frequently discussing the challenges we were facing. That group became a lifeline for me. Even so, although I outwardly appeared to have an unshakable faith, the seeds of skepticism had been sown in me, and over time they would be watered and begin to sprout.

You can imagine my shock when, at the end of the semester, that same professor asked to meet with me after class. On a bench outside, underneath the moss-laden oak trees, we had a friendly visit in which he asked some additional questions about my faith. This time, however, they were questions of genuine interest. As we talked, he admitted that he actually *didn't* have all the answers and that he had personally struggled with his own issues of faith. I can't say that he became a believer, but gone was the cocksure attitude that he had previously displayed before the class. *Man,* I thought to myself, *I wish the class could see him now.* But for him, that would mean letting down his guard in public and allowing his students to see his vulnerability, a risk he wasn't going to take.

I learned something deeply profound that day, something that has stayed with me my whole life. Not everything is as it seems. We must always question what people tell us and challenge our assumptions. Whether it is a professor or a preacher, an atheist or a believer, we can't simply swallow what people are saying as truth. It behooves us to listen to their arguments politely, but then test them to see if they hold water or not. A lot of people sound like they know what they are talking about and have convinced themselves that they know what they are talking about, when in reality, they don't. This is especially true in our politically correct, culturally relevant, media-driven society. I'm not saying that there are not incredibly intelligent people out there who don't believe. There are, but many of them also battle with insecurities and doubts about their own beliefs. They just don't want you to know they struggle. As you will see in this book, quite often it takes as much faith or more for them to believe their ideas.

Romans 1:22 states, *"Professing to be wise, they became fools."* There are a lot of people out there who profess to be wise, who have a list of degrees behind their names and have even written bestselling books, but they are foolish in their reasoning. My first mistake in college was assuming that my professor knew what he was talking about, that he was somehow superior in intelligence to me and to those in my life, like my parents, grandparents, and pastors, who had helped lay my foundation of faith. Certainly they couldn't have as much wisdom and insight as he. I assumed, because he was a professor at a major university, that his arguments must be sound and based on rational thinking and proven facts. I also assumed that he was correct in his assessment that to be a Bible-believing Christian you had to take this giant leap of blind faith into unreason. Was I ever wrong!

A BELIEVING SKEPTIC? IS THAT POSSIBLE?

When I tell people that I'm a skeptic, they often raise their eyebrows in question. This is the case because most who know me know that I am outspoken and serious about my faith. I've been a Christ-follower for thirty-five years; I went to seminary; I pastored a church; I have counseled many in the faith; I have written numerous faith books; I have done countless interviews on Christian radio and television; and I have spoken to scores of Christian groups. God is absolutely real to me and is the core reason for my existence. I've often asked myself what I would do if it could be proven unequivocally that God didn't exist. The answer is: I would be devastated. I'm betting the farm that He does.

So, how can one be a skeptic and at the same time a committed believer? Usually the words *skeptic* and *believer* don't go together. It's an oxymoron. But actually it's more common than you may think. In fact, I maintain that most believers at times struggle with skepticism and doubt, but are afraid to say it. To them, admitting this means a serious lack of faith with which God is certainly not pleased. Yet I contend that when we are honest about our skepticism and questions (as if God didn't know), they can become tools in God's hand to lead us into a deeper, stronger faith.

Consider Thomas, one of Jesus' twelve disciples. After Jesus had been crucified and raised, the other disciples saw Him and relayed this fact to Thomas. But Thomas couldn't believe without proof. He was skeptical and wanted solid evidence. And what did Jesus do? Jesus didn't demean Thomas for a lack of faith; rather, He appeared to him, let him touch His side, and then said to them, *"…Do not be unbelieving, but believing.…Blessed are those who have not seen and yet have believed"* (John 20:27,29). It goes on to say that, *"…Jesus did many other signs in the presence of His disciples…"* (John 20:30). He gave them evidence and miraculous experiences to encourage and confirm their faith. We give Thomas a hard time for doubting, but Thomas' faith became so strong that he died as a martyr.

On another occasion, a man came to Jesus and cried out with tears, *"Lord…help my unbelief!"* (Mark 9:24). Again, Jesus did not respond with condemnation, but answered the man's prayer by healing his son. I'm not saying that skepticism is a virtue and that God will always answer our prayers the same way as He did this man or Thomas, but when we honestly bring our skepticism to God and diligently seek truth, He will not condemn us, but will help us find it. But we must diligently seek truth with an honest, open heart. While writing this book, I heard the story of a young man who had set out to disprove Christianity, and in the process, he became a believer. He said that the whole time he was conducting his research, he was telling himself, "I don't want it to be true. I don't want it to be true." Of course, he was willing to honestly observe the facts despite his personal perceptions.

Beginning in Journalism school, this seed of skepticism was planted and began to grow silently and stealthily inside me. Though I was a believer, like a pebble in my shoe, doubt about certain aspects of my faith irritated me enough to cause me to ask hard questions and seek factual answers. At first, my doubts arose from the arguments that science and academia were throwing at me. Then, over the years, as I began to experience more of life's ordeals and became more involved with ministry, I started seeing a lot of additional "stuff" to make me question my faith at times. Allow me to explain for a moment—and rant a bit!

The people who have hurt me the most in life have been professing Christians. The people who have been the most dishonest and manipulative to me have been Christians. It amazes me how some Christians can stretch and twist the truth, selectively remembering what they want and conveniently slanting it in their favor. I've seen Christians who are supposed to be representing Christ on Earth do the most stupid things that leave unbelievers mocking and me cringing. Christians can be some of the most self-absorbed, self-righteous, self-promoting people I know—often thinking they're speaking for God when in reality they are speaking from their own self-centered, self-created agendas, not from the Spirit of Christ. Much evil, misrepresentation, and sheer goofiness has been done in the name of religion and, unfortunately, in the name of Christianity.

I've seen pastors and pastor's wives have affairs with members of their congregations, ripping churches and whole families apart, leaving a wake of destruction in their path. I've seen a church secretary convicted of fraud for stealing money from the denomination. I know a man who, as a teenager, was scolded by the religious leaders for going to a rodeo and got kicked out of church for wearing blue jeans. He's wrestled with faith and his view of God ever since. Fifty years later, even women now wear blue jeans in that church! What caused the change? I'm quite sure it wasn't God. God never cared about blue jeans in the first place! A woman once came to me crying because she was worried about going to hell for cutting her hair. Let me just say, for the record, that the God I know would never send someone to hell for cutting her hair. Such ideas are ludicrous, insane, and just bad theology. It amazes me that people actually buy into such nonsense, and it's astounding what these people will do to try to be accepted by God. More than just a few times, I've been shocked and deeply disappointed by Christians and religion.

Now, lest you think that I'm just Christian and Church bashing, I suppose I'm more disappointed with my *own* failures than anyone else's. I can't tell you how many times I've fallen short of the Christian standard. I'm quite certain that there are those who would read these pages and say, "Yeah Max, I can really relate to what you're saying. You're the one who disappointed me!" Being disappointed and undone with myself time and time again has often left me wondering about my own faith.

Then there's God. Why does He so often seem to be silent when we're hurting the most? For example, my son James was born deaf. He's now twenty-four. It's been a long, hard struggle. Not long ago, he and I were having lunch together. James had just turned eighteen; he was bright and handsome, full of dreams. He looked up at me with wet eyes and spoke to me in sign language, "Daddy," he signed. "I've asked God to fix my ears again and again and again and nothing happens. Why? Does God not know sign language?"

"James, son," I signed back, my heart ripping out, eyes pressuring from the tears. "If I could, I would take my own ears and give them to you. But I can't." I sat there and thought, *The one thing my son desperately wants and the one thing I desperately desire to give him is the one thing I am absolutely powerless to do anything about. It's out of my control.* Everyday, not some days, not every other day, but every single day I live with this nagging pain of knowing my son is suffering, that life is a constant uphill struggle for him. And some days it just about takes me down. It's one thing for you to experience pain, but to see your child suffer—sometimes that's almost too much to bear.

As an author who speaks to people from all walks of life, I regularly come in contact with hurting and disillusioned people who have experienced everything from divorce, to disease, to having multiple children killed. The plain hard truth is, life is difficult, people are hurting, and many are asking questions like, "If God is real and supposedly loves me so much, then why did He allow this? How can a good God allow such bad things? How can I trust God or even believe in God?"

Why is my son deaf? Why did 180,000 people die in a tsunami and 200,000 in an earthquake? Why does God allow tyrannical government leaders to execute tens of thousands of innocent people?

Why does the institutional Church seem so irrelevant, and why do Christians disappoint so much? Why do I fail so often?

GOD THE MASTER PLANNER AND JOURNALISM

God is a master planner. He is constantly working and orchestrating, using things in our lives even when we don't know it. Back in 1979, after I graduated from high school, I was young, zealous, and naïve. Although I loved football, my heart was set on seminary and doing ministry. But because I had a football scholarship to the University of Mississippi, my parents and I felt it would be in my best interest to take advantage of the opportunity—a free education! Dad never belittled my desire for ministry. Instead, he told me that if I still wanted to pursue ministry after undergraduate school, then he would help pay for my additional schooling, but only if I got my degree first. That sounded reasonable to me.

I chose Journalism in part because I needed a major and also because I felt it would help develop my writing skills before seminary. I never intended to work as a journalist. Really, I just wanted to get through undergrad school as fast as I could and get to seminary. Little did I realize, however, that over the course of my life, it would be the tools I learned in Journalism that would become central to who I am. Not only have I used my journalism skills when researching and interviewing people and ghostwriting their books, but these skills have played a critical role in the development and increase of my faith.

Journalism is about observing, interviewing, researching, and reporting. It's about questioning assumptions and getting facts. Perhaps my journalistic tendencies increased my skepticism, causing me to question things a bit more, but it was the tenacity for getting the facts that I learned in Journalism that would be used to strengthen my faith. Because I've been a skeptic and questioned the assumptions that have been thrown my way, both from the secular and Christian worlds, like doubting Thomas, God has graciously allowed me to see things that have lead me to the deepest, richest faith I could ever imagine. There have been the dark nights of the soul when in anguish I have cried out to God, "Help me in my unbelief!" and He has always responded overwhelmingly. He's brought me from questioning the sanity of my belief to understanding the absolute *Insanity of Unbelief.*

This book is about questioning assumptions and looking at the facts. My goal is to present valid rationale for beliefs that have profoundly changed my life and then let you make your own decisions. I also want to be upfront with everyone, especially my non-believing friends. I do have an agenda. It is to encourage those struggling in their faith, to strengthen believers. I do not apologize for being a Christian. Everything you read in this book is based on solid, honest reporting. I will not hold back on my critique of weird, exaggerated claims that Christians often make, but neither will I throw the baby out with the bathwater.

Whether you think your faith is unshakable or you have little or no faith, don't be afraid to ask hard questions and get convincing answers. Cry out, "Lord, help me in my unbelief!" God can take it. He wants to hear from you and will respond to your cry. Then allow the truth to enlighten your mind so you'll have an answer to the onslaughts that unbelievers and life throw your way.

Chapter 2

SOME PRETTY GOOD COMPANY

"I think it's pretty much agreed that all that God business is out the window." Dismissing the topic as easily as he tipped the chair back from the seminar-room table, our senior colleague continued his brief, articulate review of the leading theories of consciousness. Who agreed to that? I wondered. Who agreed to that? —Dr. Linda S. Schwab, Center for Brain Research, School of Medicine and Dentistry, University of Rochester[1]

The following statement appeared in my hometown newspaper's opinion section some time back:

MANY PEOPLE DON'T TRUST IN GOD

Like many taxpayers and citizens of this country, I do not trust in God. In fact, many have come to accept *the fact that there is no such thing as God.* God is a myth—a fairy tale, a kind of Santa Claus figure; comforting to children and useful in controlling the gullible masses.

We might just as well post "I believe in the tooth fairy" on our walls...

I have tried to guide my children in their journey toward becoming responsible, *ethical adults by emphasizing facts, not fiction; provable science, not faith-based malarkey.* We place our trust very carefully upon ourselves, our family, and good friends. We trust our public officials to a point; we trust our police department. I trust my dog. This trust was earned by virtue of repeated, reliable, observable behavior. *I am truly astounded by those who continue to trust in God.*[2]

The above writer has very emotionally bought into several assumptions. Namely, that belief in God is faith-based malarkey founded on fiction, not provable facts of science. He goes on to say that he was "truly astounded by those who continue to trust in God." Unfortunately, the society in which we live has been inundated with this type of assumptive ideology. When my daughter was in high school, her science teacher announced to the class, in a mocking sort of way, that "no serious scientists believe in God or Creation." This was a popular, highly-touted, award-winning teacher. The impact of statements and ideologies like these can be lethal to one's belief, especially when they are reinforced by the media and Hollywood.

I'll get back to this teacher, but let's talk about popular movies and television for a moment. For the most part, producers have done a masterful job at portraying believers in a negative light. Rarely, if ever, are Christians made to appear intelligent, enlightened, mentally-balanced, or on the cutting edge of culture. In most films, a character of faith is depicted as loony, hypocritical, or judgmental and is positioned at odds with another character who is well-balanced, somewhat skeptical, and of course, logical. Guess who wins out? If average people were to look to movies and television for their view of people of faith, we'd all look like narrow-minded buffoons or insensitive bigots. In an article entitled "Why Hollywood Hates Christianity" in the *FrontPageMagazine.com,* Don Feder wrote:

Since at least the 1970s, Hollywood's treatment of Christians has been only slightly more benevolent than al-Qaeda's attitude toward Jews. Gone are the kindly Barry Fitzgerald priest, the wise rabbi and the steadfast minister. In their place is a rogue's gallery of lusting priests, sadistic nuns, perverted pastors and con-men TV evangelists – not to mention ordinary Christians (Catholic or evangelical) who are depicted as superstitious nitwits, malevolent hypocrites, or both.[3]

The combination of Hollywood's mentality with the anti-faith ideology that much of academia touts is a double-edged sword that has created a culture of unbelief and cynicism. They actually feed off one another. For those who are on the fence spiritually, who are skeptical and uninformed, it's all too easy to jump on the bandwagon of unbelief. The problem is, the ideology is just not true. It's based on false assumptions. Whether he believed what he was saying or not, what my daughter's science teacher told the class that day was an outright lie. When we dig deep and challenge these assumptions by observing the *real* facts instead of just swallowing what the culture and some scientists and educators are saying, we can come to quite a different conclusion. Not only do intelligent people believe, but some of the *most* intelligent people believe.

My goal in this chapter is not to present evidence and arguments for the existence of God. There are other books already written by more qualified writers that do that. I merely wish to refute the claim that belief in God and being a person of faith is simplistic, unscientific, and non-intellectual by letting you hear what some of the most brilliant minds in the world, both past and contemporary, have to say about the subject. Some you will recognize; others you won't. Please pay careful attention to their credentials and the institutes of higher learning they come from. These are not preachers; they are top scientists and philosophers. Note that I am not saying that they are all Christians, though many are, but merely that they acknowledge a superior intelligence that governs creation. This chapter is out of the norm because it contains such a large number of quotes. I felt it was necessary, however, to lay a solid foundation for the rest of the book. Personally, I could read quotes forever. Finally, in an effort to dispel what some call "quote mining," I have attempted to find direct statements that would be difficult to be construed as out of context.

BRILLIANT MINDS OF OLD

The supreme God exists necessarily, and by the same necessity He exists always and everywhere...He endureth forever, and is everywhere present; and by existing always and everywhere, He constitutes duration and space...In Him are all things contained and moved.[4]

When I lay my [telescope] aside, go into my room, shut the door, and get down on my knees in earnest prayer, I see more of Heaven and feel closer to the Lord than if I were assisted by all the telescopes on earth. —Sir Isaac Newton[5]

The proof in favor of an intelligent God as the author of creation stood as infinity to unity against any other hypothesis of ultimate causation; that it was infinitely more probable that a set of writing implements thrown promiscuously against parchment would produce Homer's *Iliad*, than that creation was originated by any other cause than God. The evidence for God as opposed to the evidence against Him as the Creator of this universe was infinity to one. It could not even be measured. —Pierre-Simon Laplace, French mathematician and astronomer whose work was critical to the advance of mathematical astronomy and statistics[6]

Everything in the world shows either the unhappy condition of man, or the mercy of God; either the weakness of man without God, or the power of man assisted by God. —Blaise Pascal, Mathematician, physicist, and child prodigy, noted for Pascal's Wager, Pascal's Triangle, and Pascal's Law[7]

We get closer to God as we get more intimately and understandingly acquainted with the things He has created...And let us hope that in the mysterious ways of the Lord, He will bring about these things we all so much hope for...Let us pray that the Lord will completely guide us in all things, and that we may gladly be led by Him... —George Washington Carver, Scientist, botanist, educator, and inventor whose studies and teaching revolutionized agriculture in the Southern United States; best known for his work with peanuts, creating over 300 products from them[8]

The scientist's religious feeling takes the form of a rapturous amazement at the harmony of natural law, *which reveals an intelligence of such superiority* that, compared with it, all the systematic thinking and acting of human beings is an absolutely insignificant reflection... I defend the Good God against the idea of a continuous game of dice.[9]

...I'm not much with people, and I'm not a family man. I want my peace. I want to know how God created this world. I am not interested in this or that phenomenon in the spectrum of this or that element. I want to know His thoughts, the rest are details. —Albert Einstein, winner of the Nobel Prize in Physics[10]

Each will have to make his own choice: to oppose the will of God, building upon the sands the unstable house of his brief illusive life, or to join in the eternal, deathless movement of true life in accordance with God's will. —Leo Tolstoy, Author of *War and Peace,* and other novels, and one of the world's greatest novelists and critical thinkers[11]

In the name of God, I William Shakespeare…God be praised, do make and ordain this, my last will and testament in manner and form following. That is to say, first I commend my soul into the hands of God my Creator, hoping and assuredly believing, through the only merits of Jesus Christ, my saviour, to be made partaker of eternal life, and my body to the earth whereof it is made. —William Shakespeare[12]

In good philosophy, the word cause ought to be reserved to the single divine impulse that has formed the universe. —Louis Pasteur, French chemist and microbiologist remembered for his remarkable breakthroughs in the causes and preventions of disease[13]

BRILLIANT CONTEMPORARY MINDS

It is not difficult for me to have this faith, for it is incontrovertible that where there is a plan there is intelligence—an orderly, unfolding universe testifies to the truth of the most majestic statement ever uttered—"In the beginning, God." —Arthur H. Compton, Winner of the Nobel Prize for Physics, former professor of physics at the University of Chicago[14]

So many essential conditions are necessary for life to exist on our earth that it is mathematically impossible that all of them could exist in proper relationship by chance on any one earth at one time. —A. Cressy Morrison, Past president of the New York Academy of Sciences[15]

Today as we ponder the unique architecture of the molecular systems that make up life, I am sure that I will not be the last person to conclude that 'there must be an architect.' I cannot possibly conceive how such a system could ever evolve. —Dr. Bob Hosken, Holds a doctorate in biochemistry, is senior lecturer in food technology at the University of Newcastle, Australia, and has published more than fifty research papers in the areas of protein structure and function, food technology, and food product development[16]

God has allowed us the privilege of living in a time when great mysteries are being uncovered. No previous era knew about quantum mechanics, relativity, subatomic particles, supernovas, ageless photons, or DNA. They all reveal the stunning genius of a God who spoke a time-space-matter-light universe into existence, balanced it with impossible requirements of precision, and then gifted it with life. —Dr. Richard A. Swenson, M.D., Physician and futurist who taught at the University of Wisconsin Medical School for fifteen years[17]

The complexity of life's biology is held within its internal processes, but dressed in the simplicity of our outer bodies. Anyone who thinks nature is simple should take a short user-friendly course in how just one cell 'evolves' into two cells, and then marvel at the vast amount of information required to bring about this single step and then wonder at its source...The hidden face of God is found in the details. —Dr. Gerald Schroeder, Earned doctorate from MIT before moving to laboratories at Weizmann Institute, the Hebrew University, and Volcani Research Institute in Israel; his work has been reported in *Time*, *Newsweek*, and *Scientific America*[18]

If we regard God's world as a site of purpose and intention and accept that we, as contemplative surveyors of the universe, are included in that intention, then the

vision is incomplete without a role for divine communication, a place for God both as Creator-Sustainer and
as Redeemer… —Dr. Owen Gingerich, Noted Harvard
astronomer, former research professor of Astronomy and
History of Science at Harvard University, and senior
astronomer emeritus at the Smithsonian Astrophysical
Observatory[19]

Many scientists do believe in both science and God, the
God of revelation, in a perfectly consistent way. —Dr.
Richard Ferriman, Winner of the Nobel Prize in Physics[20]

It seems to me that when confronted with the marvels
of life and the Universe, one must ask why and not just
how. The only possible answers are religious…I find a
need for God in the Universe and in my own life. —Dr.
Arthur Schawlow, Professor of physics at Stanford University and winner of the Nobel Prize for Physics[21]

We would never expect, for example, a box of Lego
bricks thrown into the air to fall by chance into a
model of the Chateau de Versailles or for my son's bedroom to become tidier without the imposition of some
miraculous force. Therefore, if the universe were formed
through purely random processes, we should expect it
to comprise nothing but chaos and not, as we see, galaxies, stars, and shopping malls. —Dr. Stephen D. Unwin,
Received his doctorate in theoretical physics from the
University of Manchester for his research in the field
of quantum gravity and has written for *New Scientist*,
among other influential scientific journals[22]

Because all forms of life contain a code (DNA, RNA),
as well as all of the other levels of information, we are
within the definition of information. We can therefore
conclude that there must be an intelligent sender…
The information encoded in DNA far exceeds all our

current technologies. Hence, no human being could possibly qualify as the sender, who must therefore be sought outside our visible world. We can conclude that there is only one sender, who must not only be exceptionally intelligent, but must also possess an infinitely large amount of information and intelligence—that is, He must be omniscient and beyond that, eternal. —Dr. Werner Gitt, Doctorate of Engineering, director and professor at the German Federal Institute of Physics, Braunschweig, from 1978-2002[23]

The first gulp from the glass of natural sciences will turn you into an atheist, but at the bottom of the glass God is waiting for you. —Werner Heisenberg, Winner of the Nobel Prize in Physics[24]

We're just working with the tools God gave us... There's no reason that science and religion have to operate in an adversarial relationship. Both come from the same source, the only source of truth—the Creator. —Joseph Murray, Winner of the Nobel Prize in Medicine and Physiology[25]

When I began my career as a cosmologist some twenty years ago, I was a convinced atheist. I never in my wildest dreams imagined that one day I would be writing a book purporting to show that the central claims of Judeo-Christian theology are in fact true, that these claims are straightforward deductions of the laws of physics as we now understand them. I have been forced into these conclusions by the inexorable logic of my own special branch of physics. —Dr. Frank J. Tipler, PhD in Physics from Massachusetts Institute of Technology, mathematical physicist and cosmologist, holding a joint appointment in the Departments of Mathematics and Physics at Tulane University[26]

As we survey all the evidence, the thought insistently arises that some supernatural agency—or, rather, Agency—must be involved. Is it possible that suddenly, without intending to, we have stumbled upon scientific proof of the existence of a Supreme Being? Was it God who stepped in and so providentially crafted the cosmos for our benefit? —Dr. George Greenstein, PhD, Yale graduate, professor of Astronomy at University of Massachusetts, Amherst[27]

There must be a cause apart from matter...a mind that directs and shapes matter into organic forms. Even if it does so by creating chemical mechanisms to carry out the task with autonomy, this artist will be the ultimate cause of those forms existing in matter. This artist is God, and nature is God's handiwork. —Dr. George Stanciu, PhD in technical physics, professor of physics at University "Politehnica" of Bucharest, director of the Center of Microscopy-Microanalysis and Information Processing[28]

Shall I go on? I could quote from literally hundreds of top scientists and thinkers. You will meet many more of them throughout the rest of this book. The truth is, some of the most brilliant, intellectual minds in the world believe that God is good science; many are Nobel Prize winners. And the more technology uncovers, the more of God we see. Many who don't believe in a Creator do so *despite* the overwhelming evidence. The following quote is from another Nobel Prize winning scientist. He's a non-believer, but at least he's honest.

I do not want to believe in God. Therefore, I choose to believe in that which I know is *scientifically impossible*, spontaneous generation arising to evolution. —George Wald, Chemist and Nobel Prize winner for medicine[29]

Friend, if you believe in God, don't let the media or any professed intellectual force you into the mold that your faith is unsophisticated, naïve, or insane. It's just not reality. The truth is, if you believe in God, then you're in some pretty good company!

I will praise You, for I am fearfully and wonderfully made; marvelous are Your works, and that my soul knows very well. —King David (Psalm 139:14)

Chapter 3

"BUT MOMMY, WHEN WAS GOD BORN?"

I find it quite improbable that such order came out of chaos. There has to be some organizing principle. God to me is a mystery but is the explanation for the miracle of existence, why there is something instead of nothing. —Alan Sandage, Winner of the Crawford Prize in astronomy[1]

"Mommy, who made the trees and the flowers and the stars?" the young girl asked with eyes full of wonder as she looked up at her mother, who was tucking her into bed.

"God did, honey," the mother responded lovingly. "He made the stars and the moon. He made Mommy and Daddy, and He made you, too."

The girl smiled contently, but then a perplexed look crossed her face. "But Mommy," she asked, "when was God born?"

A perplexed look then crossed the mother's face. "It's time to go to sleep now, honey," she said and kissed her daughter goodnight.

If you are breathing, then the odds are great that you have at one time or another asked the little girl's question. If we are created by

God, then who created God? And it's also likely that you handled it much like the mother did—just sort of pushed it aside because you didn't have an answer and the thought was too much to comprehend. Thinking about it for long can make our brains feel like mush. The question is bigger than us. We find it difficult to wrap our minds around the concept of eternity and of an eternal being because all we've ever known is this time-space continuum. Yet this question and others like it tug at us, almost wooing us. We want to know, and I believe we do because the tug was placed there by God Himself. Ecclesiastes 3:11 says, *"...He has put eternity in their hearts, except that no one can find out the work that God does from beginning to end."* In other words, we'll have this tug toward God, this innate knowing that there's something bigger than ourselves, and God does promise to reveal Himself to those who diligently seek Him (see Heb. 11:6), but at the same time, we will never fully grasp the magnitude of His being with our finite minds while we're on this Earth. As the apostle Paul said,

> *We can see and understand only a little about God now, as if we were peering at His reflection in a poor mirror, but someday we are going to see Him in His completeness, face to face...* (1 Corinthians 13:12 TLB).

All we can hope for in this dimension is to get glimpses, clues of His existence and majesty. This holds true for me, you, and the smartest scientists or philosophers on the planet.

When it comes to comprehending God, the greatest scientific minds and the little girl's mind are not that far apart. After all the research, testing, and theories are said and done, it boils down to childlike questions and the reality of our limited knowledge. Einstein himself couldn't have said it better.

> We are in the position of a little child entering a huge library filled with books in many different languages. The child knows someone must have written those books. It does not know how. The child dimly suspects a mysterious order in the arrangement of the books but

doesn't know what it is. That, it seems to me, is the attitude of even the most intelligent human being toward God. We see a universe marvelously arranged and obeying certain laws, but only dimly understand these laws. Our limited minds cannot grasp the mysterious force that moves the constellations.[2]

Jesus said that we must *"become as little children"* in order to enter the kingdom of God or to even begin our understanding of God (see Matt. 18:3-4). This childlike place is not a place where we cease to reason, but is a place of humility. Intellectual arrogance only leads to more insanity and lack of understanding. *"The fear of the Lord,"* Proverbs says, *"is the beginning of knowledge..."* (Prov. 1:7). The word *fear* in this passage denotes a reverential respect or awe. It's an understanding that God is God and we are not. Having said that, this childlike humility and acknowledgement of the in-comprehendible vastness of God does not mean that we are to abandon our critical thinking. Critical thinking from observing reality and testing our assumptions can actually help us arrive at a logical, commonsense conclusion that supports God's eternal reality, and that it is quite sane, not insane, to believe in a self-existent being who is outside of time.

IF ANYTHING EXISTS, SOMETHING MUST BE SELF-EXISTENT

The very fact that we exist, or that anything exists, *demands* that something is self-existent. That is, it has the power of being within itself—that it wasn't created and is timeless. Even though it blows our minds and we can't comprehend it, logic requires it. There is no other way. From bacteria to buffalo, everything that exists in the universe is made of matter/energy. Either this matter/energy has always been around (is self-existent and eternal) and evolved into the fine-tuned universe that presently exists, or God, who is self-existent and eternal, created matter/energy and is the intelligence behind the universe's order. It has to be one or the other because spontaneous generation from absolute nothingness is impossible. If there was ever a time when there was absolute nothingness, then it is impossible for something, anything at all, to exist. Think about it. Something can't come from true nothingness. Remember our quote from the previous chapter by Nobel Prize winner George Wald? "I do not want to believe in God. Therefore, I choose to believe in that which I know is scientifically impossible, spontaneous generation arising to evolution."[3]

Dean Overman, author of *A Case for the Existence of God*, says,

> To be rational the atheist must show how something comes from nothing. Otherwise, the existence of something is not explained...One has to have a starting point, and if an atheist is not going to beg the question why her starting point exists, she must begin from really nothing—what Francis Schaeffer called nothing-nothing.[4]

At the risk of sounding overly repetitive, I'll say it again. Something, anything, a puff of energy, a speck of matter, cannot come from nothing-nothing. Therefore, something had to have always been! An eternal something is necessary for us to be here.

This very point was one of the reasons former world-renown atheist Antony Flew recanted his atheism. Flew has written dozens of books in support of atheism, including such titles as, *God: A Critical Inquiry*, *Darwinian Evolution*, and *Atheistic Humanism*. In England, he spent twenty years as professor of philosophy at the University of Keele, and he has also held positions at Oxford, the University of Aberdeen, and the University of Reading. He was arguably the best-known atheist in the English-speaking world until his announcement in 2004 that he now accepts the existence of God. In his 2007 book, *There is a God: How the World's Most Notorious Atheist Changed His Mind,* Flew states the following:

> Can something come from nothing?...My two main antitheological books were both written long before either the development of the big-bang cosmology or

the introduction of the fine-tuning [of the universe] argument...But since the early 1980's, I had begun to reconsider. I confessed at that point that atheists have to be embarrassed by the contemporary cosmological consensus, for cosmologists were providing scientific proof... that the universe had a beginning...If the universe had a beginning, it became entirely sensible, almost inevitable, to ask what produced this beginning...If there is to be a plausible law to explain the beginning of the universe, then it would have to say something like "empty space necessarily gives rise to *matter/energy*."...Jim Hartle, Stephen Hawking, and Alex Vilenkin have speculated that the universe quantum-fluctuated into existence "from nothing."...[But] Hawking had, in fact, noted *the need for a creative factor to breathe fire* into the equations...

Richard Swinburne [author of *The Existence of God*] summarizes his exposition of the cosmological argument by saying: "There is quite a chance that, if there is a God, he will make something of the finitude and complexity of a universe. *It is very unlikely that a universe would exist uncaused, but rather more likely that God would exist uncaused.* Hence the argument from the existence of the universe to the existence of God is a good argument." In a recent discussion with Swinburne, I noted that his version of the cosmological argument seems to be right in a fundamental way...The universe is something that begs an explanation.[5]

Coming to the same reasonable conclusion as Antony Flew doesn't take a degree in Physics or Philosophy. It's simply a matter of observing the world around us with childlike wonder, awe, and commonsense reasoning. Two thousand years ago, the apostle Paul stated what many scientists and philosophers are discovering today,

For since the creation of the world His invisible attributes are clearly seen, being understood by the things that are made, even His eternal power and Godhead... (Romans 1:20).

So, here's the deal. After we observe the world around us, we have to choose where to place our faith. Either in (A)—the building blocks of the universe, matter/energy, were self-existent and eternal and evolved by random chance into the staggeringly complex order that we find today, including making the accidental leap somewhere along the timeline from non-living to living beings with emotions and moral thought. Or, in (B)—God is self-existent, eternal, and is the intelligent force behind the development and fine tuning of the universe. It *is* either A or B because it is impossible for something to come out of absolute nothingness. There was never a time when nothing existed. I ask you: Which one requires more faith to believe?

Read what Dr. Stephen C. Meyer, who earned his PhD from Cambridge University, said about our complex world coming into being by chance:

> While many [scientists] outside origin-of-life [fields] may still invoke "chance" as a causal explanation for the origin of biological information, few serious researchers still do...Chance is not an adequate explanation for the origin of biological complexity and specificity... Our experience with information-intensive systems indicates that such systems always come from an intelligent source—i.e., from mental or personal agents, not chance...During the last forty years, every naturalistic model proposed has failed to explain the origin of information...Thus, mind or intelligence or what philosophers call "agent causation" [intelligent designer], now stands as the only cause known to be capable of creating an information-rich system, including the coding regions of DNA.[6]

It seems apparent that the more commonsense, rational view is to place our faith in (B)—that God is self-existent, eternal, and the intelligent force behind the development and fine tuning of the universe. And the answer to the little girl's question of "who made God?" is "nobody." God always was. Does that sound familiar?

In the beginning God created the heavens and the earth (Genesis 1:1).

I am the Alpha and the Omega, the Beginning and the End, the First and the Last (Revelation 22:13).

All things were made through Him, and without Him nothing was made that was made (John 1:3).

For by Him all things were created that are in heaven and that are on earth, visible and invisible...He is before all things, and in Him all things consist (Colossians 1:16-17).

By faith we understand that the worlds were framed by the word of God, so that the things which are seen were not made of things which are visible (Hebrews 11:3).

Chapter 4

DO BONA FIDE, PROVABLE MIRACLES STILL HAPPEN TODAY?

You say you have experienced God directly? Well, some people have experienced a pink elephant, but that probably doesn't impress you…That is all that needs to be said about personal 'experiences' of gods or other religious phenomena. If you've had such an experience, you may well find yourself believing firmly that it was real. But don't expect the rest of us to take your word for it, especially if we have the slightest familiarity with the brain and its powerful workings. —Richard Dawkins, *The God Delusion*[1]

To sum it up in a nutshell, Richard Dawkins, along with other famous atheists such as Sam Harris (author of *The End of Faith)* and Christopher Hitchens (author of *God is Not Great)* are convinced that a person who believes in a personal God who speaks and does miracles is nothing short of delusional. Sam Harris went so far as to say that believing in a God who communicates specifically is "demonstrative of mental illness."[2] And apparently, these guys have quite a loyal following. All three of their books were *New York Times* bestsellers.

Not long ago, I was talking with a young atheist. He was in his early twenties, extremely brilliant, annoyingly arrogant, and viscously angry at anything that remotely resembled faith in God. We were having a friendly debate on the existence of God until I came to the subject of miracles. When I started to tell him one woman's incredible story (one that is in this chapter), he adamantly rejected it, *not* wanting to hear the details of the event. So much so, that he walked out of the room. To him, personal stories are invalid because they are emotional, subjective, and usually fabricated in the person's head. "There's no way an experience can be proven," he said.

As I write this chapter, I am acutely aware that many unbelievers and skeptics will roll their eyes in ridicule. Some will have the same response as my young atheist friend. They simply do not want to hear it because they have made up their minds that miracles just don't happen and that any report of a "supposed" miracle is an emotional delusion or an outright fabrication. They're convinced that some people want to believe so badly that they create scenarios in their minds to confirm their beliefs. As a result, their brains sometimes play tricks on them, or they find themselves gullibly falling for fairy-tales. The unbelievers and skeptics commonly make statements like, "I believe that *you* believe a miracle occurred." Of course, they make such statements in a patronizing way, as if they are much more grounded, intelligent, and enlightened.

MY OWN SKEPTICISM ABOUT MIRACLES

To give credit to the skeptics, over the past thirty-something years of ministry, I have personally seen a lot of weird, questionable, and delusional stuff. Sometimes people *do* want to believe so badly that they create scenarios in their own minds. They also will search out stories to confirm what they want to hear. And I must confess that much of the time when someone says to me that "God" told them something, I inwardly roll *my* eyes. I've often wondered about people who claim miracle healings in these big crusades for things like runny noses or headaches when there are those present with real problems who don't get healed, like paraplegics or the deaf and blind. Christians are notorious for getting so caught up in the emotion of telling a "God" story that they quite often stretch the facts and sometimes lie. Even though I'm passionate about my faith and can get emotional, I detest misinformation and embellishment.

I get confused and even angry whenever I hear of some super-zealous, ignorant, religious nuts who have withheld medicine or treatment from their child because of faith in God and the child dies. I get angry at the parents and confused at God. Even though the parents are wrong for withholding the medicine, the kid is innocent, and you'd think God would honor that.

And talking about delusions—I once knew a woman whose doctors declared was unable to have children; she prayed to God for a miracle pregnancy. Then, when her stomach began to grow, she announced to everyone that God had miraculously touched her womb and given her a child. She told her parents, her friends, anybody who'd listen. Baby showers were thrown, gifts were given. She even gave her testimony before a large church. Everybody rejoiced at the incredible miracle of God. But when she became ill and almost died, the doctors removed a tumor from her abdomen the size of a baby. It was the largest tumor in the hospital's history! But here's the real kicker. She knew all along that it was a tumor, even when it was just a pebble of a thing. Yet she wanted a miracle so badly that she believed God was going to miraculously turn the tumor into a fetus. She thought by confessing in faith that it was a child, God would do it. She also thought that acknowledging the truth and going to the doctor for treatment of the tumor would be showing a lack of faith. So she merely deceived people, including her husband and parents, justifying her actions in the name of God. Now that's delusional and it's also unethical.

I've also seen more than my share of unanswered prayers of the faithful. A while back on an airplane, I sat next to a precious young couple. It was obvious that the wife was battling cancer, yet her positive countenance almost overshadowed the fact. The couple was returning from M.D. Anderson Hospital, where she had undergone a series of chemotherapy treatments. Both were strong believers with a faith and optimism that was contagious. They proudly showed me a picture of their two beautiful children. We had a wonderful time of fellowship and felt the Spirit of God heavy upon us during the plane ride. When it was time to depart, we all three held hands and prayed. I felt a special anointing and prayed for her healing. It was a powerful encounter. They gave me their address, and once home, I sent them some of my books. A week or so later, I received a delightful thank you letter. The letter also noted that the pain had started getting unbearable and she had been reduced to a wheelchair. In the privacy of my office, I once again prayed for her recovery. A few weeks later, she died.

My friend Johnny Nicosia was the type of person who challenged people to live better just by being around him. God's love and grace oozed from him in a most authentic way. If there was anyone who didn't deserve to get a brain tumor, it was him. Hundreds of people prayed for Johnny, and he never gave up his trust and faith in God. He also died.

I ghostwrote a book for a pastor of a 20,000 member church who believed strongly in the power of prayer and healing. While I was writing the book, he was battling terminal Non-Hodgkin's Lymphoma. The pastor chose to go forward with the recommended treatment, while claiming his healing by faith. Prayer vigils and prayer meetings were held on his behalf. Literally thousands upon thousands of people from all across the globe interceded for his healing. But in the end there was no miracle, and he died in his fifties. I could go on and on with similar stories. And don't forget, I have a deaf son whom we've prayed over countless times through the years with nothing, nada, not a thing. He's still just as deaf as he's ever been. It's as if, at times, God simply ignores the cries of some of His most faithful followers. C.S. Lewis captured the feelings of many when he penned the following in his book *A Grief Observed*.

Meanwhile, where is God? This is one of the most disquieting symptoms. When you are happy, so happy that you have no sense of needing Him, if you turn to Him then with praise, you will be welcomed with open arms. But go to Him when your need is desperate, when all other help is vain and what do you find? A door slammed in your face, and a sound of bolting and double bolting on the inside. After that, silence. You may as well turn away.[3]

Now, please understand. It is not my intention to be the bearer of doom and gloom or to squash anyone's faith. I believe by the end of this book your faith will be stronger than ever before, whether you've experienced a miracle or not. The point I'm trying to establish is that, just like most people, I often don't understand God's ways and neither am I someone who is out of touch with reality. Yes, I believe God works in miraculous ways, but miracles are clearly *not* the norm. If you have a headache, you take an aspirin. If you have diabetes, you watch your diet and take your medication. Can God supernaturally heal diabetes? You bet He can. As you will see in the rest of this chapter, God is very much alive today and *is* personally involved in our lives. Despite all of the exaggerations, false claims, and prayers that seemingly went unanswered, my personal faith is stronger than it has ever been because of what I *have* seen God do. God still does real, bona fide, provable miracles.

MY JOURNALISTIC INSTINCT

One of the reasons my faith has grown deeper despite some of the negative things I've seen is because of some of the incredibly miraculous things I have seen. I took it upon myself to question the assumptions that this skeptical society has tried to tell me about miracles. Over the years, I've asked God to lead me to real, authentic miracles, and He has overwhelmingly answered my prayer. As a result, what I found to be true was the *exact opposite* of what the high-profile atheists are chanting. They are the ones who have become delusional because, in their attempts to discredit authentic miracles and anyone's faith in God, they have not pursued or fully examined the details. I agree wholeheartedly with Fyodor Dostoevsky when he wrote,

> A true realist, if he is not a believer, will always find in himself the strength and ability not to believe in miracles, and if a miracle stands before him as an irrefutable fact, he will sooner doubt his own senses than admit the fact.[4]

Keep in mind that this book was not written for those who do not want to hear, but to encourage believers and those whom God is drawing to Himself. There will always be skeptics and unbelievers, even from the religious community. The Bible clearly states, *"...for not all have faith"* (2 Thess. 3:2). When Jesus did His miracles, many believed; however, there were also many who didn't believe. *"But although He had done so many signs before them, they did not **believe** in Him"* (John 12:37). I've even heard well-meaning preachers and supposed scholars say God doesn't do real miracles today. I would tell them the same thing I tell the atheist. If you think God doesn't do real miracles today, then you haven't looked hard enough because, I assure you, He does. It is amazing what you can find when you dig for it, but you have to really want to find it. I think that's the way God intended it.

Remember, God rewards those who diligently seek Him (see Heb. 11:6). And there is a difference between diligently seeking truth in an unbiased way versus trying to find information simply to support your beliefs. My goal in this chapter is to encourage your faith by establishing that legitimate, provable miracles are occurring today. To do this, I've approached the following three miracle accounts in a skeptical but unbiased way, putting them through a series of journalistic criteria.

- Is the account so startling and odds-defying that *miraculous* is the only possible way to describe it? Is there any possibility that it could be chance or a trick of the mind? Can it only be described as an act of God?

- Are the people involved of reliable character and of a sound mind?

- Is documentation available that establishes the facts of the story?

- Has the story been exaggerated or fabricated?

- Are there reliable witnesses?

If the alleged miracle failed any one of the above criteria, then it was not considered for this chapter.

BONA FIDE MIRACLE #1

The Marolyn Ford Story: A woman's complete and instantaneous healing of blindness after prayer

Marolyn Ford's dramatic, on-the-spot, instantaneous healing of blindness as a result of a specific prayer is a miracle of such magnitude that, if authentic, holds deep implications for our own lives. Of course, if merely an exaggeration or fabrication, it wouldn't carry any implications at all. For this book, I knew that simply reading about her story from another source wouldn't cut it. The only way to satisfy my own personal skepticism would be to conduct a face-to-face interview where I could ask tough questions and get straight answers. If there were any holes in the story, any stretching of the truth or fabrication, I was determined to find out.

Because Marolyn's miracle occurred thirty-eight years ago in 1972 (a detail that, as you will see, actually gives more power to the story), I was not sure that she was still alive or would even agree to such an interview. To my surprise, however, I found both Marolyn and her husband, Acie, still very much alive and active, residing in Memphis, Tennessee. Interviewing Acie was an added benefit because he was the one who prayed for her when she was instantaneously healed. After numerous telephone conversations and e-mail correspondences, the Fords graciously agreed to open their home to me. The following is the result of that five-hour interview. After you read, you can decide for yourself what to believe.

In this story, I've attempted to present the data as a journalist would by systematically establishing: 1) credibility of character, 2) the truth and extent of Marolyn's blindness prior to the alleged miracle, 3) the detail and description of the miracle itself, 4) the events following the miracle, including reactions of witnesses, 5) documentation, and 6) summary and conclusion.

Upon my arrival at the Fords' residence, it was snowing outside, and I was greeted by two warm, down-to-earth people. Acie, in his early seventies, was unassuming and humble. He was returning from hospital visitation where his ministry is to counsel and pray with the sick and their families. Marolyn, in her late sixties, had bright eyes beaming with energy and a vivacious spirit that was infectious.

The Fords had spent their lives serving others through their church work in North Louisiana, Southern Arkansas, and Tennessee. At the time of the interview, Acie was working as an associate pastor at the Broadmoor Baptist Church in Memphis, where he is actively ministering today. My first impression was that these people were hardly the type who would lie or make false claims intentionally. They were far more interested in talking about Jesus than promoting themselves. If they told a miracle story, it was because they truly believed it and desired to glorify God.

In 1959, at the age of eighteen, Marolyn Ford began to lose her central vision. One day, while working at her secretarial job in Holland, Michigan, everything abruptly went blurry. Distraught, she frantically relayed what was happening to her co-worker, Gertrude. Gertrude pointed to a woman who had just entered the room.

"Can you see her?" Gertrude asked.

"No," Marolyn responded. "I can't see that far!" The woman was only about fifteen feet away. In a two day period, Marolyn went from normal eyesight to almost total blindness. She could no longer drive, work, or do most of the everyday activities that just days before she had taken for granted. Marolyn was devastated.

Over the next several months, she was in and out of numerous doctors' offices and underwent a plethora of tests. Eyeglasses didn't help, and no one could tell her what was wrong. Eventually, Marolyn ended up at the Mayo Clinic in Rochester, Minnesota, which had the premier eye clinic in the nation at that time. The final diagnosis was Juvenile Macular Degeneration. The doctor concluded that there was no treatment available. He told Marolyn bluntly, that the best thing she could do would be to "go home and learn to live with it." On the following page is a letter from the Mayo Clinic confirming Marolyn's diagnosis.

When considering Marolyn's miracle, keep in mind that, based on the above report, her best correctable visual acuity was 7/200, 14/224 in each eye. I took this letter to a local ophthalmologist and asked what it meant. The doctor responded, "It means she's practically blind, at least legally blind with very little light perception." According to the Snellen Visual Acuity chart, 14/224 meant Marolyn had a 92.8 percent loss of eyesight when the original diagnosis was made. The doctor then explained to me that 7/200 meant the smallest letter Marolyn could read at seven feet could be read by a normal eye at two hundred feet. With what sight she had, she could only make out vague outlines, no detail. When I read the letter to the doctor and his two assistants and then told them that the lady now has perfect vision, they all three said it was impossible to recover from macular degeneration, and that if true, it would have to be a miracle. According to *The American Medical Association Encyclopedia of Medicine,* macular degeneration destroys the retinal nerve tissue and replaces it with scar tissue, and the disorder is untreatable. That is, once the retinal nerves are destroyed, spontaneous remission is impossible.[5]

As one might imagine, being legally blind, with her eyesight getting progressively worse, the years following were difficult. Yet Marolyn continued to trust God and never gave in to a victim mentality. Determined to move on with life, she attended Tennessee Temple University where President Dr. Lee Roberson provided

Mayo Clinic

Rochester, Minnesota 55901
Telephone 507 282-2511

Robert W. Hollenhorst, M.D.
Ophthalmology

2-303-077

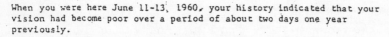

Visual Difficulties
began in 1959

Mrs. Marolyn Ford
Box 266
Huttig, Arkansas   71747

Dear Mrs. Ford:

When you were here June 11-13, 1960, your history indicated that your
vision had become poor over a period of about two days one year
previously.

Examination of your eyes showed a best correctable visual acuity of 7/200,
14/224 in each eye. This decreased vision was due to a dense central
scotoma in each eye caused by a yellowish area of atrophy in the macular
retina of each eye. A diagnosis of juvenile macular degeneration was made.
We were unable to offer any treatment.

A general physical examination gave normal results except for mild diffuse
enlargement of the thyroid. All tests for thyrotoxicosis were, however,
normal.

Yours very truly,

Robert W. Hollenhorst, M.D.

RWH:kro

Marolyn with tapes for her reel-to-reel tape recorder so she could study by listening to the class lectures, since she couldn't read the class books. It was during her time at Tennessee Temple that she met Acie Ford. Even though Marolyn was blind and never saw his face, the two dated and fell in love. Eventually, they were married and began working as a husband and wife ministry team. Acie was a pastor and Marolyn did music. Soon they had a daughter named Sharon who, like her husband, Marolyn loved dearly, but couldn't see. Thirteen years passed.

Then, while they were serving as pastors of Crossroads Baptist Church in Farmerville, Louisiana, Marolyn began to lose what remaining eyesight she had. At that point, she could no longer make out the big "E" on the eye chart. Marolyn had a four-finger count in one eye and hand motion in the other. That meant when a hand was held up, she could make out four fingers, and when a hand was waved inches in front of her face, she could make out the movement. Again, no detail—just outlines. But now, that was rapidly leaving her too. Her vision had failed to the point where she only had some light perception. She could see movement and light through windows and doors. That was about it.

Marolyn's condition became so desperate that she had to leave her family for a period of months to attend the Arkansas Enterprise for the Blind in Little Rock to receive further training. It was at the AEB that she learned how to read Braille, walk with a white cane, and do math on a Chinese bead-board called an abacus. During my interview, Marolyn demonstrated the Braille technique. It was obvious that she knew what she was talking about. After she came home from the blind school, Braille tags were attached to all sorts of things. For example, they were sewn in the hems of garments to indicate color, and she used cooking utensils that had Braille markings on the measuring spoons. Marolyn presented several photos of her reading Braille to her daughter and of her walking with her cane.

A man by the name of John Strickland was her Mobility Instructor. It was his job to train Marolyn to learn how to be an independent blind person. One story involving her Mobility Instructor stuck out for me. Once he lit a cigarette lighter and held it about six inches from her face. Marolyn never knew it. She did pick up the heat and smell and asked Mr. Strickland if he was smoking. He told her what he had done and why. He did it to see the severity of her light perception. Basically, she had none. The document on the following page verifies that Marolyn Ford attended the Arkansas School for the Blind. The record is old and worn, so you might have to strain a bit to make it out, but it was the best the school had.

The point of all of the above is to establish the truth that Marolyn Ford was indeed blind and indeed attended the Arkansas Enterprise for the Blind. Now, I ask, why does a person attend a blind school, learn to read Braille, learn to walk with a cane, and learn to function as a blind person? It is because they are blind. This may seem over-simplified, but if Marolyn wasn't blind, the school would have known it and would not have allowed her to attend.

THE MIRACLE

On the evening of August 25, 1972, thirteen years after Marolyn's initial diagnosis of Macular Degeneration, believe it or not, on Acie's thirty-third birthday, the miracle occurred. That night, driving home from visiting Acie's family, the couple had talked in depth about their struggles, particularly those involving Marolyn's blindness. They were able to talk more that night because Sharon had asked to stay and sleep with her grandparents. Life had been unusually rough as they had fought with Marolyn's increasing blindness. Both Marolyn and Acie were overwhelmed to the point of despair. After the long and exhausting day, the two were finally ready to turn in and get some much needed sleep. The time was about 1:00 a.m.

Acie told me that Marolyn had climbed into bed. Despite the late hour and their fatigue, Acie read a short devotion and then slipped

Arkansas Enterprize for the Blind

REPORT ON EYE EXAMINATION

(TO EXAMINER: PLEASE RETURN TO THE REFERRING OFFICE)

(12-9-40)

APPLICANT'S NAME: Mrs. Marilyn Ford   AGE   SEX F   RACE W

ADDRESS: Route 2, Farmerville, Louisiana   PARISH Union

EYE HISTORY: Retinal disorder OU.

Degeneration and scarring of
Sharula in both eye

DIAGNOSIS (Primary Cause): Exotropia 10 to 15 Foram Dioptek
Macular Degeneration
Legally Blind

RECOMMENDATIONS: None

CENTRAL VISUAL ACUITY

F.C. IS Finger Count

	Without glasses		With best correction	
	Distance (20 ft.)	Near	Distance (20 ft.)	Near (14 in.)
R.E.	FC	FC	20/400	FC
L.E.	HMHM	FC	FC	

PRESCRIPTION FOR GLASSES

	Sphere	Cylinder	Axis	Add	Vision
R.E.	None				
L.E.					
Presently worn R.E.	75	-50	175		
L.E.	2.50	-50	175		

Is binocular function present? ☐ Yes ☒ No

Date of Examination 4/29/71

Date of Report 2/17/71

Signature of Examiner

Original sent to State Office and 2 copies sent to Miss Ford on his knees beside the bed. He laid his hands across Marolyn as she lay there. They both began to cry as with great feeling and desperation. Acie prayed a simple prayer. "Oh, God!" he cried out. "You can restore Marolyn's eyesight, Lord. I know You can. And God, if it be Your will, I pray You will do it tonight." Suddenly, after thirteen years of blindness, there was sharpness and light! Laying there in her bed, as her husband prayed, Marolyn's sight was instantly and perfectly restored! Because of my own skepticism, I asked Marolyn to go over again with me exactly what happened in her words.

"Well," she said, "When Acie began to pray, I had closed my eyes."

"That's kind of strange," I said, "I mean, a blind person closing their eyes to pray. Don't you think?"

"Oh, no," she responded. "Even though I was blind, I had trained myself to close my eyes for prayer. It was just something I did naturally because I wanted to look and act as normal as possible."

"What was the difference with your eyes open and when they were closed?"

"There was little difference," she said. "When my eyes were open, all I saw was a gray haze. Before I had closed my eyes that night, I couldn't see anything, but when I opened my eyes after Acie had prayed, to my amazement, I could see perfectly. There he was, right there in front of me, the husband I had never seen before!"

Acie said that it wasn't a case of great faith because he was shocked and couldn't believe what was happening. "It was all God's doing."

"Acie, I can see!" Marolyn shouted. "I can see!"

"What do you mean, you can see? You're kidding?" Acie shouted back.

"I can see the pupils of your eyes, and I can see your rosy cheeks! Acie, it's 1:00 a.m. You need a shave! Acie, I can see!"

Acie still couldn't believe that a miracle had really occurred so he ran into the other room and grabbed a copy of the *Monroe Morning*

World newspaper. He held it up in front of Marolyn and asked if she could read the large print.

"I can do better than that!" she exclaimed. "I can read the fine print!"

The couple praised God all night. Even though it was the wee hours of the morning, they called both Marolyn's parents and Acie's, waking them up for the news. Marolyn ran around the house examining things, especially Acie and her own self in the mirror. Imagine not seeing yourself for thirteen years! Over and over again she looked at the photo of Sharon, which had been setting on the dresser. It was one of the most joyous moments when, the next day, Marolyn finally saw her daughter face-to-face. Not too long afterward, Marolyn and Acie made a trip to Holland, Michigan, especially so Marolyn could see what her family now looked like. While there, she shared her miracle with the Immanuel Baptist Church in Holland as a sighted person. Ironically, she had also spoken at that same church earlier as a blind person.

Nearly everyone in the community and surrounding areas where they lived in Louisiana knew of Marolyn's blindness. She had shopped at the local stores with her white cane in hand and had recently spoken for the local Lion's Club as a blind person. The Lion's Club is known for their work with the blind. When word got out about the miracle, literally hundreds of people flooded to the Fords' home. Though Acie and Marolyn were pastors of the Crossroads Baptist Church, people from all the churches around came to see—Pentecostals, Catholics, Methodists, and even people of no faith. It was such news that several newspapers picked up on the story.

Later that week, when Marolyn went to the eye doctor, he revealed that an even greater miracle had occurred. The doctor's startling report indicated that her eyes, medically speaking, had not changed at all. The macular was still full of holes, and the nerve endings were still dead. The doctor acknowledged that it was impossible for her to be seeing, yet she could see. Some time later, Marolyn was attending a funeral, and the eye doctor's assistant happened to be there. She pulled Marolyn aside and told her the following story.

She said, "Marolyn, you don't know me, but I have to tell you what happened the day you came in to see the doctor after your miracle happened. My job was to follow the doctor back into his office after he saw a patient, and he would dictate to me what to write down on the patient's medical record. I would take it in shorthand and then later type it out. Well, that day, after the doctor told you that he didn't know what you were seeing with, we went to his office, and he sat in his chair, leaned back, and just sat there in total quietness. This went on for like twenty minutes, and I started to feel really uncomfortable, not knowing whether I should leave the room or wait for his dictation. Then finally, he looked up and said, 'I don't know what that lady is seeing with. I don't know what to tell you to put on her record. I've never seen anything like it.'"

So, here's the deal. It is an established historical fact that Marolyn Ford was blind and that she attended the Arkansas Enterprise for the Blind. She learned to read Braille, walk with a cane, and so forth, something one does not do if she can see. There were hundreds of witnesses who knew she was blind. Likewise, there were hundreds of witnesses who confirmed her healing, not the least was her own husband and daughter. Even Mr. Strickland from the blind school came and visited.

If Marolyn was not genuinely blind, why did Acie even pray for her that night? And if she could see anything before he prayed, why would he run and get a newspaper to test her sight after he prayed? But here's the real kicker that proves to me that this is a bona fide miracle of God. For thirteen years, Marolyn was blind and was so up until the moment of the prayer. There was a very specific prayer asking for her healing. She closed her eyes as a blind person and opened them as a sighted person with perfect vision. Was it a coincidence that her eyesight just happened to return the moment of the prayer? After thirteen years? You tell me.

Finally, as I talked with this well-documented once blind lady, it was obvious to me that, at nearly seventy, she could see quite well, better than me! I need glasses; she does not. On the following page is a letter from Dr. David G. Evans, O.D. of Memphis, Tennessee.

The bottom line is that Marolyn Ford had a miracle of biblical proportions, and the only way a person can deny it is to choose to flagrantly disregard the obvious. That, my friend, would be pure insanity. This lady's experience is not, as Richard Dawkins says, "a pink elephant" or a result of "the brain and its powerful workings." It is ridiculous to conclude that Marolyn Ford received her sight as a result of wishful thinking or the powers of the mind. Nope, a woman was blind, her husband prayed, and she got a miracle as a sovereign act of God.

Roy Brunson had been a vice-president of a Fortune 500 company, a multi-millionaire, and a hardcore atheist. Raised as an atheist, his mother drilled into him that a God who allowed evil in the world couldn't possibly exist. Then one day Roy's glorious life came crashing down. I'll spare you the details, but he found himself broke, devastated, angry, and contemplating suicide. Today, Roy Brunson heads up World Light Ministries and is an evangelist/ missionary to the Ukraine and Africa. At last count he has led over 215,000 people to faith in Christ. What happened to change his mind? He credits sitting next to Marolyn Ford on an airplane as the single event in his life that was the catalyst to his salvation and rebirth. Listen to Roy's own words:

> I was on a plane from Dallas to Memphis contemplat-
> ing how I would take my own life, when an attractive,
> middle-aged woman sat next to me. After some small
> talk, she could tell something was bothering me. "Jesus
> loves you," she said with a warm smile. "Lady," I shouted
> back, "exactly what did God do for you anyway?" That
> was a mistake. She told me she had been totally blind
> for over thirteen years. One night after coming home
> from visiting relatives, her husband, who was a Baptist

"See the best you can see"

David G. Evans, O.D.

Don W. Gayso, O.D.

Eugene B. McLaurin, M.D.

Elizabeth W. Mitchell, M.D.

John E. Linn, M.D.

Howard L. Beale, M.D.

• Comprehensive Eye Examinations

• Glaucoma Specialty Care

• No Stitch/No Needle Cataract Surgery

• Diabetic Eye Care

• Laser Vision Correction

• Dry Eye Treatment

• Clinical Research

• Fashion Eye Wear

• Contact Lenses

6060 Primacy Parkway
Suite 200
Memphis, TN 38119

Phone: (901) 761-4620
Fax: (901) 761-3072

www.totaleyecarememphis.com

September 11, 2007

To Whom It May Concern:

Re: Marolyn Ford

Mrs. Marolyn Ford has been my patient for six years and I can report that today, Mrs. Ford has 20/30 visual acuity in both eyes. This is only two lines from 20/20, which is considered perfect vision.

I have reviewed her previous medical records on multiple occasions, which date back to the early 1960's. At that time, she was legally blind with visual acuity of "finger counting" in the right eye and "hand motion" in the left eye.

In my fourteen years of practice, I have never experienced this type of profound visual acuity improvement with any patient. Certainly, with today's modern surgical procedures, a physician can offer visual improvement to many patients. However, in this case surgery was not an option and was never offered.

It is my opinion that the Ultimate Physician was at work in 1972 when this miracle occurred. I believe that God is still doing a miracle in the life of Mrs. Ford today.

In His Service,

David G. Evans, O.D.

minister, got down on his knees and started praying for her eyesight while she lay in bed. She said he prayed, "God, I know that You can make Marolyn see. O God, make her see now" and just like that she saw her husband Acie for the first time. Then she saw her daughter for the first time. She had met and married Acie while she was in college when she was blind. She then went on to explain that she had numerous doctors examine her and they all said it was impossible for her to see. The damage to her eyes was still there and beyond repair. But they could not explain how she now had 20/20 vision. They had to admit that the only explanation possible was a supernatural one. It could only be a miracle. Her blue eyes looked right through me into my soul. I was very frightened. Could my mother be wrong? Was there really a God that loved me and had a plan for my life?[6]

BONA FIDE MIRACLE #2

The David Yaniv Story: A former atheist, paralyzed for seven and a half years, experiences a medically impossible instant healing after a specific word of knowledge

David Yaniv has a long, documented history with strong endorsements. In 2010, he was appointed International Ambassador for the Messianic Israel Alliance. The organization states that they chose David because of his outstanding character, humble heart, and lifetime of courage. When I first talked to David and Sheila Yaniv, I was immediately drawn in by their humble, warm, and unassuming manner. I could see why they had been bestowed such an honor. Like Acie and Marolyn Ford, when I spoke personally with David and Sheila Yaniv, they too seemed more interested in promoting Jesus than themselves. And as you will see in this story, their miracle actually cost them quite a bit.

DAVID THE ATHEIST

Retired Colonel David Yaniv was not only a soldier in the Israeli military, but he was also an outspoken, Jewish atheist. But how can one be both Jewish and atheist? He was Jewish in heritage, but atheist in belief—a secular Jew. Born in Tel Aviv in 1936, after his parents had emigrated from Nazi Germany, David and his family regularly celebrated Yom Kippur, Rosh Hashanah, Hanukah, and other Jewish holidays. After WWII, however, when David's father got news that his two sisters, a brother, and their families had been brutally massacred by Hitler, he rid the house of every Tanach (Jewish Bible), along with anything else remotely religious.

"Where was God?" he would shout. "How could God allow such things to happen?" He never set foot in a synagogue again, and from then on, it was drilled into young David's head that there was no God. How could there be? For the next several decades, until the late 1980s, David waved the banner of his father's atheism. "I was never, ever religious," David said. "I thought people who believed in God were nuts. I did not believe in God at all." Yet today, David Yaniv is a devoted follower of Jesus Christ and the pastor of Roots Messianic Congregation outside of Seattle, Washington. What made the difference in this once hard, skeptical atheist? The answer is an encounter with the living Christ and a bona fide, modern-day, documented miracle.

It's a miracle that, when examined honestly, leads to only one reasonable conclusion: It was a supernatural act of God. For people to *not* believe, they would have to blatantly disregard the overwhelming body of evidence. Unfortunately, though, many will do just that. When I was interviewing David, he told me that he was constantly amazed at how some people could hear his story, see the vast evidence, and still refuse to accept it. I believe it's because many skeptics have their minds already committed to unbelief. They have so much invested in their own worldview and lifestyle that they feel they can't or don't want to change. Anything that threatens their view they automatically reject, often throwing out insulting and even hateful comments instead of honestly considering the claims. When doing research for this book, I came across a plethora of degrading comments by unbelievers. The following example is a blogger's response to another man's book dealing with supernatural accounts similar in nature as this one. The comment sums up my point pretty well.

> I can understand religion being in people's lives to make them feel secure and protected by a "higher being," but when you say things like this I feel the need to argue it, because lying even more than you already are is pathetic...that is just garbage and BS...You know, I know, and so do any knowledgeable people that these stories aren't true...I guarantee!...[People who believe these stories] are the same kinds of people who say they have seen ghosts of their family members, or have been abducted by an alien spaceship, because these kind of things do not happen. If people claim they do, experts should go see them because they are hearing things, and seeing things and going a little haywire...People always tend to say "it was God's doing" when they have no explanation for something. This is just lack of knowledge...[7]

Instead of seeking out the facts, people like this make arrogant, absurd, and unsubstantiated statements. I happen to know the author of the book that this commenter was accusing of lying, and he is a credible man who has done his homework. Another example of this type of absurdity is what Christopher Hitchens wrote in his memior, *Hitch-22.* He said,

> I try to deny myself any illusions or delusions and I think that this perhaps entitles me to try and deny the same to others, at least as long as they refuse to keep their fantasies to themselves.[8]

My interpretation of that comment is, "I don't want to think about, consider, or even hear anything that might possibly persuade me from my commitment to unbelief. So if you try to tell me of an experience, I'm going to shoot down your claim by calling you delusional." Statements and mindsets like these are just plain ridiculous. Why would someone want to deny and not even look into the possibility of a claim being true? After all, isn't truth what we all want? One would think so, but unfortunately reality confirms otherwise. Many tout intellectual integrity when what they exhibit is the ultimate in arrogance that is not intelligent at all. It's actually rather *insane*. David Yaniv's miracle account in the next several pages is no delusion or fantasy. It *is* the real deal.

A DOCTOR'S MISTAKE

During this time, David, Sheila, and their two sons lived on a moshav in Israel. A moshav is a type of cooperative agricultural settlement similar to a kibbutz. It's like a small town with stores, gas stations, a medical clinic, and so forth, except everyone shares chores, finances, benefits, and the yield. One day, while shoveling in a cowshed, David slipped on a wet spot and fell flat on his back. Because he was in so much pain, he went to the hospital in Tel Aviv to have it checked out. After a special X-ray called a mylogram, it was concluded that he had two slipped discs, and he needed corrective surgery. The neurosurgeon, however, assured David that it was a routine operation and nothing to worry about. "Ten days," he said, "and you'll be back home as good as new."

David had the operation, except it turned out to be anything but minor *or* routine. When he awoke from the surgery that evening, David had no feeling from the waist down. At first, the doctor on call thought the paralysis was only temporary due to swelling around the spinal cord, but later the next day, the actual neurosurgeon explained that during surgery he had made a terrible mistake. He had cut too deeply with his scalpel, severing the nerves that were essential for David to walk, and that he would be paralyzed for life.

With one slip of the doctor's hand, David Yaniv went from a strong, robust, ex-military man to an invalid. From the hospital, he was sent directly to a convalescent home called Beth-Levinshtein, which helped paralyzed people, mainly soldiers who got wounded in the war. For three and a half months, he learned how to function as a paraplegic. David was equipped with iron calipers (braces), which were attached to special shoes. With the help of crutches and the calipers, he could make his way around without a wheelchair, although it was very difficult. He also had a catheter attached because he couldn't feel if he needed to relieve himself. Eventually, David returned home to the moshav to find his home rearranged. Friends had made a ramp for easy access into the house with his wheelchair. They also installed handles in the bathroom and other places around the house where he would need them. David was extremely grateful to his friends, yet he was very angry. "Life had become overwhelming," he said. "I hated everybody. I blamed everybody. But worst of all, I absolutely hated myself and could not accept what had happened. I was the most miserable person imaginable. I couldn't forgive the doctor. I couldn't forgive anyone. I was bitter, truly bitter."

Over the years, David tried everything he knew to change his situation. At one point, he became so desperate he even went to a guru and experimented with transcendental meditation, but nothing worked, and his condition only worsened. Life was difficult on Sheila as well. At one point, David was afraid she might leave him, but she never did. Like a devoted wife, she stuck by his side through thick and thin, offering help and encouragement the best way she knew how. But after seven and a half years of trying everything the world had to offer, David finally resigned to being a paraplegic for the rest of his life. By then Sheila, too, had given up hope that his condition would ever improve. She would say, "What are you running after? Accept it. This is how you are going to remain. I've accepted it. Why can't you?" A strong woman, she said those words in love, thinking her husband must throw out any fantasies of getting better and get on with reality.

THE MIRACLE

The doctors may have given up hope. David and Sheila may have given up hope, but God had not. One day when David was home with the flu, he was watching television and happened across a program on Lebanese television called *The 700 Club.* He had never heard of the program and thought it was an entertainment-type show because it had the word *Club* in the title. David soon discovered that it was a Christian show. Because he was bored and there was nothing else to do, he kept watching. After a while, he became intrigued. "I felt like I was doing something wrong," said David, "so I locked the door. I didn't want my wife and my children to catch me watching Christian television."

As David watched, the show continued to hold his interest because it featured stories from people who had been healed. The first time he watched, there was an interview with a woman who had been healed of cancer. She showed an X-ray of a tumor the size of an orange. Then she showed an X-ray of the same spot taken three days later. The tumor had disappeared. "I was sure it was phony," he says. "These people *had* to be paid actors." Still, David found himself watching day after day, but he did it in secret. He would roll his wheelchair to the door and lock it so Sheila and his sons wouldn't know.

During each program, there was a time of prayer, and the co-host would invite the television audience to pray along. At that point, David clicked the television off. On this one day, however, it was as if the Spirit of God was reaching out from the television set directly to him, prodding him to pray along. The next thing David knew, he was praying to receive Jesus into his life. "Afterward, I couldn't believe what I had done!" he said. "What on earth do I do now? I was sure I was the only Jewish person in the world who had ever prayed that prayer."

Yet God's Spirit continued to deal with him. Though he couldn't explain it, David knew he'd experienced something real. Soon he purchased a Bible and started reading it and growing in his faith.

"As I started reading my Bible," he said, "I soon discovered there was more to it than I had ever imagined. I found that the prophecies from the Old Testament are fulfilled in the New Testament. And I started to wonder why Jewish people throughout the centuries had not believed in Jesus."

When David finally told Sheila, he wasn't sure how she would react, yet she responded more positively than he'd expected. "If it makes you feel good, you just carry on," she said. "But do me a favor. Don't tell anyone about it. Let it be between us for now."

About five months after David became a believer in the Messiah, he was again watching *The 700 Club* when co-host Danuta Soderman had what some Christians call a word of knowledge.

"There is someone watching who has been paralyzed halfway down his body for years," Danuta said. "He will feel a warm sensation running through his body, and he will be healed."

"Oh, please, God, let it be me," David cried out. He believed the word of knowledge was for him, but nothing happened. "I felt my legs, and they were still as unresponsive as they had ever been. Yet I kept praying because I figured if it wasn't for me, it must have been for someone else."

Little did David know, however, that the word of knowledge actually was meant for him. Listen to what happened in his own words.

> That same evening around ten o'clock I was lying in bed reading a book, when all of a sudden a feeling like an electric current ran from my spine down to my tiptoes, and my feet started jumping out of control I imagine about forty or so inches in the air. I didn't know what was happening and really couldn't explain the electric shock. Finally, the spasms stopped, and I went to sleep.
>
> The next morning, I woke up feeling like I had a full bladder and needed to go to the bathroom. I thought this was strange because for seven and a half years I had

not felt the urge to urinate. I had to go to the hospital regularly to get my catheter cleaned. I started to assist my legs with my hands as I usually did, in order to get them out of bed. As I touched my legs, all of a sudden I realized I had feeling in them! I started to touch all the places where I had lost feeling years before. There was feeling in them!

"Sheila!" I shouted, "For God's sake, come here! I can feel!"

"Rubbish," she said. "Lie down." She took a needle and started pricking me. "Close your eyes. Where am I pricking you?" She continued pricking me in different places on my legs. Each time she pricked my legs, I told her the correct spot. Now she began to share my excitement.

That very morning, the couple went to the dispensary on the moshav to see the doctor. David put his special shoes back on because he still didn't know exactly what had happened. Plus, after seven and a half years of paralysis, his legs had severe atrophy. When the moshav doctor was shocked too, David and Sheila realized a true miracle had occurred. The moshav doctor sent him back to the hospital in Tel Aviv for an electric test of his reflexes. This test had been done many times before on David, and the results were always negative. But this time his reflexes responded to the test perfectly! The doctor who performed the test asked David if he could return the following week.

A week later, David and Sheila met with about twenty-five doctors, neurosurgeons, and neurologists from all over Israel, including the neurosurgeon who had operated on him. In the end, not one could give a logical explanation for what had happened. They all agreed it was not possible. A couple of doctors even accused David of lying by claiming that the older X-rays were not his. To this day, doctors who examine him cannot believe he is walking. At the end of the examination, the doctors told David it was a "medical miracle."

"Listen," David told them. "This is not a medical miracle. This is Yeshua, Jesus."

"That was too much for these Jewish doctors," David said. "They didn't want to hear another word about this 'Jesus.' They refused to believe He could have had anything to do with my healing. We know from the Bible that even when people saw Jesus perform miracles right before their eyes, some didn't believe. Some even accused Him of being demon possessed."

Afterward, the doctor told David he could stop using his iron calipers (braces) and his wheelchair, but to keep using the crutches because his legs were just skin and bones. Ever so slowly, David took his first steps in seven and a half years. "I walked out of the hospital with all my calipers and everything in the wheelchair, pushing it with legs that were so thin. Because of seven and a half years of atrophy, they had no muscle and were just fragile, skin and bone. I knelt down on knees that hadn't felt anything since the accident and thanked the Lord for the miracle He had done."

But God wasn't finished with David yet. The doctors had told him that the muscles in his legs were all dead and that they would never grow back. Over time, however, God recreated those muscles. Today, David's legs and feet are just as normal as anyone else's.

Because his body had been made whole again by an undeniable miracle, David and Sheila were eager to share the wonderful news with all who would listen. But being a Christian on a Jewish Israeli moshav proved difficult. The Yanivs were told to stop telling people about Jesus, and in 1988, after a series of painful events, they were voted out of the moshav and were given ten days to vacate. The Yanivs had lost everything—their home, their jobs, their friends, and a relationship with their youngest son, all in one month. And because all the money in the moshav is pooled, no one has any personal savings. This left David and Sheila financially destitute as well—all because they would not renounce their faith in the God who had healed him—Yeshua, Jesus. God, however, used this situation for their good, and David and Sheila were presented with a full scholarship to Christ For the Nations, a Bible school in Dallas, Texas. They moved to Dallas with nothing, only a trust in God to provide for them and show them His will for the rest of their lives.

HERE'S THE DEAL

Fact #1: David Yaniv was indeed paralyzed. It's a medically documented fact, not a "made-up story." Medical records show it. Witnesses could testify. He's a credible source with many who endorse his story.

Fact #2: For seven and a half years David had tried everything to get better. If he could have gotten better through other means, such as positive thinking and "the brain and its powerful workings," as Dawkins suggests, he would have. The electricity running through his body and the jumping around of his legs were totally outside his realm of thinking or his own power. He wasn't expecting it. He was lying in bed reading a book. David also would have had corrective surgery if it would have helped. But surgery wasn't an option because the doctor had severed the nerves. They were irreparable.

Fact #3: After seven and a half years of being wheelchair-bound, he just happened to get his feeling back after a prophetic word of knowledge saying that someone paralyzed from the waist down for years is being healed and he "will feel a warm sensation running through his body." That same night, he felt an electric current (warm sensation) running through his body, and he woke up with complete feeling. I'd like to see a mathematician put some numbers to that!

Fact #4: Twenty-five doctors, neurosurgeons, and neurologists examined him and concluded it was a "medical miracle."

Fact #5: As a result of the healing, David and Sheila had a complete lifestyle change, including being kicked out of the moshav and losing family and finances, all because they wouldn't stop declaring Jesus Christ. They are now pastors of a church. Typically one doesn't make those kinds of sacrifices for a known lie. David and Sheila knew that Jesus had healed him and that he owed his walking and salvation to Him. That's why they were willing to lose everything, even family, rather than deny what they knew was true.

ONLY OPTIONS FOR UNBELIEF

Option #1: *David and Sheila Yaniv are honest, but mistaken.* That argument doesn't fly. David had no feeling. He couldn't walk. The people he lived around everyday knew it. Then, overnight, he had feeling in his legs and even in his bladder. Where did the feelings suddenly come from? It's kind of hard to mistake something like that.

Option #2: *They are outright lying and making the whole thing up.* Nope. That doesn't fly either. There are too many witnesses who can easily testify that it is not a fraud. David has told his story for years, and no one has discredited him. They are not lying, and it is ridiculous to even consider that option. On top of that, they had nothing to benefit from making this story up. Why fabricate something that causes you to lose everything and become destitute? Plus, the obvious fact is that David could suddenly walk after being unable to for seven and a half years.

Option #3: *It's an exaggerated claim.* Nope. That doesn't fly either. The medical professionals were baffled. Twenty-five doctors, neurosurgeons, and neurologists examined him. Plus, David had tried everything to walk, and nothing had worked. When Danuta Soderman gave the word of knowledge, David still had no feeling in his lower body at that moment. He felt himself to see if he was healed, but nothing had happened. If even some feeling had come back, he would have tried to walk. Instead, David went to bed discouraged, but that night the miracle occurred when he wasn't expecting it.

Option #4: A person simply does not want to accept the facts and chooses to disregard them.

Considering all of the above, the only rational conclusion is that David Yaniv experienced a modern-day miracle of biblical proportions.

BONA FIDE MIRACLE #3

The Bruce Van Natta Story: Surgically removed organs restored supernaturally after specific prayer

In February of 2007, thirty-six-year-old Bruce Van Natta lay in a hospital bed dying, his body wasting away. At five-foot-nine-inches, he normally weighed a robust 180 pounds, but now, being fed intravenously, he was down to about 125 and was rapidly declining. Several months earlier, on November 16, 2006, Bruce had been in a terrible accident when a six-ton logging truck he was working under collapsed on top of him. Bruce's chest, abdomen, and pelvis were crushed under the truck's axle, and five major arteries were severed. By all rights, he should have died on the spot, but God seemed to have other plans. Bruce had a life-altering, out-of-body experience in which his spirit hovered above the scene of the accident, and he viewed himself being frantically worked on by the EMTs. Afterward, he was able to recount specific details of the event that he could not have possibly known because he was unconscious when they occurred. Oh, and there's another thing. While he was out of his body, Bruce encountered two stunning angels, one on each side of his injured body, with their arms under the truck, keeping him alive.

When personally interviewing Bruce, I asked if his out-of-body experience was like a dream. "No way," he responded. "It was the most real thing I've ever experienced in my life. Whenever television reenactments of my experience have been done," he continued, "they usually show a haze or clouds around me. But it wasn't like that at all. Everything was clear, crystal clear, especially the angels, just like I'm looking at you right now."

Firefighter Shannon Cila was the first responder on the scene.

"Immediately I knew it was extremely serious," she said. "He had internal bleeding and internal damage. Blood was coming from his mouth. If one of the major arteries in the abdominal area is severed, you can die extremely quickly because those are the biggest veins that you have. He didn't appear to be breathing, and his skin was ashen. His eyes were closed. It looked like he was already gone. When the ambulance finally took him, I didn't expect to see him again."[9]

While Shannon was leaning over him, holding his head up and patting him in the face, trying to get some sort of response, Bruce's spirit suddenly shot back into his body. "I blinked open my eyes and was looking directly in her face," he said, "but when I closed my eyes again, I could feel my spirit slipping back away from my body. Then a quiet voice, like a whisper, told me that if I wanted to live, I would have to fight, and it would be a hard fight. All I could think of was my wife, Lori, and our four children. I decided that I would not shut my eyes and would fight for them."

Bruce was sped to a local hospital and then airlifted to the University of Wisconsin Hospital in Madison, the largest trauma center in the state. As the ER was scanning him for internal injuries, Bruce's blood pressure dropped to zero. At that point, he lost consciousness and was rushed to the operating room. According to the hospital records, when the doctors opened him up, they found the superior mesenteric artery and vein completely severed and separated, as well as other critical blood vessels that were transected and bleeding. There was 1,500 milliliters of blood pooled and clotted in his abdomen. Then he lost at least that much more in surgery. The total loss of blood was somewhere between 3,000 to 4,500 milliliters or 6 to 9 units. The average adult has approximately 8 to 10 units of blood. The team worked furiously on the blood vessels, removing the badly injured ones and reattaching the arteries that had been severed. In the process, they suctioned out at least three quarts of blood.

In addition to the severed arteries, Bruce had broken ribs, frac-
tured vertebrae, a damaged pancreas, and the majority of his small
intestines had been pulverized into mush. The ruined small intestines had to be surgically removed and the remaining pieces joined
together. His abdomen had swelled so badly from the trauma that
they could not close him up and instead packed his insides with
gauze. After a massive blood transfusion, he was taken to the ICU
to see if he would survive the next six to eight hours. If he lived, they
would go back in the next day and begin the rest of the repair work.
The doctors, however, did not offer much hope. The chief resident
surgeon told Lori that, in all his years as a trauma doctor, he had
never seen anyone so badly traumatized and still live.

But to everyone's amazement, especially the doctors', Bruce did
live. Against incredible odds, ten days later, he opened his eyes to
find Lori right there by his side. The very first thing Bruce did when
they took the tubes out of his mouth was to tell her about the angels
he'd seen. Lori had come to the hospital the night of the accident
with only her Bible and had not left since. She'd spent the majority of the time crying out to God for a miracle. Not only was Lori
praying, but a whole community of churches, family, and friends
joined in, and it seemed their prayers had been answered. Bruce
had miraculously survived the severing of five major arteries without bleeding to death; multiple internal injuries; and four surgeries
where he was cut from ribcage to pelvic bone. And he had awakened
from his coma. All of this was good news indeed, yet Bruce's battle
was far from over. He had a long, hard struggle ahead of him. Little
did Bruce know, however, that his most amazing miracle was yet to
come. It's a thoroughly documented miracle that, when the facts are
honestly examined, is impossible for even the hardest of skeptics to
refute—the supernatural restoration of Bruce's surgically removed
small intestines after specific prayer. The remainder of this chapter
is dedicated to the exploration and verification of that miracle.

Bruce Van Natta's story has been written about extensively,
yet I felt in order to maintain the integrity of this book and its

journalistic nature, I needed to interview him personally as I did with Marolyn Ford and David Yaniv. I wanted to ask tough questions and scratch below the surface. If I could uncover anything to discredit his claim, the story would not be included in this book. In addition, I sought to squeeze out any supplementary information not covered in previous reports that I felt would add to the story. The following account is the result of several personal interviews with Bruce, medical experts, and other key individuals, along with my own research and review of the medical records.

Yes, Bruce was still alive, which astounded the doctors, yet because of the inadequate amount of small intestines, he had to be fed intravenously and was slowly dying due to deficient nutritional absorption. His frail and weak body had wasted down to about 125 pounds. From mid-November of 2006 to mid-February of 2007, Bruce had a total of four surgeries, all involving the small intestines. The Surgery Notes state that a small portion of his duodenum and all but 75 centimeters of his jejunum and 25 centimeters of his ileum were *surgically removed*. When intact, the jejunum is about 250 centimeters in length, and the ileum is about 400 centimeters, for a total of about 650 centimeters or 20 to 21 feet. That means 18 to 19 feet of Bruce's small intestines were surgically removed, leaving him with only a total of 100 centimeters or 3.2 feet to function with. Then, during the fourth surgery, another 5 centimeter piece was removed, leaving him with only 95 centimeters or 37 inches. Howard LeWine, MD, at Harvard Medical School, said,

> Normal adults have about 20 feet of small intestine. To absorb sufficient calories and nutrients, at least 5 feet of small intestine would need to be saved. If less than that is able to be saved, a person would only be able to survive with intravenous feedings.[10]

The small intestines are divided into three sections, the duodenum, the jejunum, and the ileum. The ileum is the longest section, accounting for three-fifths of the small intestines. In Bruce's case, the majority of his ileum was removed, which made his situation

even more complicated. Removal of parts of the jejunum and duodenum can often be tolerated since the ileum can compensate for
some of the work they would do. But removal of the ileum, or most
of it, causes extra problems since it's responsible for the absorption of
fats, bile salts, and vitamin B12. One day, Bruce asked an attending
physician when they were going to fix him up with a colostomy bag.
A colostomy bag is a container worn on a person's side to receive
waste discharged through an opening in the abdomen. At that point
tubes were attached to Bruce's abdomen, just draining his waste
into a black pail. The physician's response to his question was, "Oh,
you're not going to have to worry about it."

"Why not?" asked Bruce.

"Bruce," the doctor said, "I'm sure you've been told already.
With the amount of intestine you have, we are just going to feed you
intravenously, and it will last about a year to year and a half before
you pass away. We just can't keep someone in your condition alive
long-term intravenously."

Bruce was devastated, and just like the doctor had predicted, he
continued to lose weight and weaken. He also got angry and confused with God. "Why would God send angels and miraculously
save my life only to let me die like this?" he told me. "It just didn't
make sense."

THE MIRACLE

Here's where the story gets really wild. It involves another man
named Bruce—Bruce Carlson, who I also interviewed personally.
At the time, Bruce Carlson, who we'll refer to as "BC" from now
on, lived in Walden, New York. Bruce and Lori had met BC about
a year prior while on vacation in New York, visiting a pastor friend
named Ryan Clark.

"It was a quick visit," BC told me. "We barely knew each other."

After the accident, news of Bruce's condition reached BC via
their mutual friend, Pastor Ryan. Then one morning in February

of 2007, while BC was getting out of bed, he felt God speak to him as an impression in his spirit. "Fly to Wisconsin, lay hands on Bruce Van Natta, and pray for his healing." Startled, BC immediately checked airline ticket prices and found that a flight to Madison was around $900. After he thought about it awhile, he told his wife, "It must have been just a crazy thought. I mean Bruce is part of a huge church with pastors and elders and hundreds of people praying. Why would God need me to fly all the way to Wisconsin and pray? It doesn't make sense for me to purchase an expensive ticket when there are already people there praying for him." At that, BC blew it off. The next morning however, the same impression came back again, only this time stronger and more persistent. "Go to Wisconsin and pray over Bruce Van Natta." BC knew it was God.

"How did you know?" I asked him.

"I knew in my knower," he said. "I just knew."

The impression was so strong that this time BC obeyed. The first thing he did after arriving in Wisconsin was meet with Bruce's pastor to let him know he wasn't trying to be some kind of spiritual superman swooping in to pray. Rather, he was simply obeying God and didn't quite get it himself as to why God wanted him to come all this way and pray.

BC entered the hospital room accompanied by Brian, another friend of Bruce's from his church. BC told me that when he first saw Bruce, he didn't look like the same person he'd met a year earlier. His eyes were sunken deep in their sockets, his skull and cheek bones protruding like someone in a concentration camp. It was obvious to BC that Bruce was dying. From this point, I want you to hear how the miracle unfolded in Bruce's Van Natta's own words.

> After greeting us, Bruce Carlson sings a couple of praise songs. I'm laying there not feeling like singing at all. After that, he just prayed a short little prayer along the lines of *"Lord I know You've heard all the prayers of all the people who have prayed for Bruce already, and I just add my prayers to those prayers. I ask that all those prayers*

would come to fruition today and heal him." Then he walked up to me and placed his right hand on my forehead. The kind of church I went to, we didn't lay hands on people like that. He started praying like Jesus prayed, which was totally different than how I had heard anyone pray before. He commanded my small intestines to grow. *"I command you to supernaturally grow in the name of Jesus."* I had my eyes closed. All of a sudden, I felt strong, high voltage electricity come out of his hand into my forehead and right down into my stomach. I actually felt electricity. It was like touching an electric fence. Zap. It wasn't emotion. It was a real feeling. And you gotta know that I wasn't expecting anything. I was in bad shape. I was weak, had no energy. I was laying there in the process of dying. Another thing, I come from a church where this kind of thing doesn't happen. All of a sudden, I began to feel my small intestines moving around. I'm not kidding. It felt like a snake uncoiled in my stomach. I actually said that to Brian and Bruce, who were in the room, "Hey, it just felt like a snake uncoiled in my stomach!"

After praying and visiting for a while, BC said his goodbyes and then flew back home to New York. Even though Bruce had experienced something powerful, he didn't understand fully what had occurred and continued to be fed intravenously. Instead of wasting away, however, he began to gain weight, which greatly confused and disturbed the medical personnel. Because he was gaining instead of losing weight, they thought something must be wrong with the IV Formula. After checking the formula, it was concluded that Bruce must have been retaining water weight. When he gained more than fifteen pounds, however, they thought something more serious was wrong and scheduled him for an upper G.I. Track X-ray exam. Listen to Bruce's own words again.

The radiologist said it was only going to take a half-hour. I had to drink this barium. After a while, the radiologist looks puzzled. He calls for my binders, my medical records. He's going through them and then calls for the senior radiologist, the head of the whole department. After looking at my records and then the new X-rays, they had me drink more barium and re-did the tests. And I can't understand why they are doing the test over. I knew something wasn't right. I can tell by the way they are acting. I hear them whispering the word *mistake* back and forth, and it scared me. They said it was nothing. I said "Oh no. If it's a mistake, I want to know what it is."

The radiologist told me, "There must be a mistake in your records because the records clearly show that you only have less than 95 centimeters of small intestines left, but according to these new tests you have at least twice that much." Later, when further tests were run, it was revealed that I actually had over 300 centimeters or nearly 10 feet! Triple what I had before.

What you have to realize is that I had had four surgeries and was cut from my ribcage to my pelvic bone four times. Each time they worked on my small intestines. So the surgeons were in there four times, and all four times, they saw my small intestines and recorded the small amount. The numbers kept being brought up in my records over and over about my small piece of intestines. Now, they're seeing at least three times that amount, 300 centimeters or 9.84 feet. That's what's confusing them. But I knew it wasn't a mistake. God supernaturally grew them out. I felt it when it happened. It felt like a snake uncoiled in my stomach.

This is science, not sensationalism. To recap, Bruce Van Natta was wasting away in the hospital, being fed intravenously because he had only 95 centimeters or 3 feet of small intestines. The other 18 feet of his small intestines had been surgically removed. The small amount of intestines remaining has been recorded in the medical records not once, but several times after four surgeries on the intestines themselves. Then a guy from New York also named Bruce flew to Wisconsin to pray because God told him to. He laid hands on him and commanded the small intestines to grow, at which point Bruce Van Natta felt electricity shoot through his body and then felt something like a snake uncoil in his stomach. Then, instead of losing weight, he started gaining weight. Confused medical personnel order an Upper G.I. Tract X-ray exam, and lo and behold, there are now at least 300 centimeters or nearly 10 feet of small intestines! Now if you are still not convinced that this is a bona fide miracle, you will be after we break down the medical records and examine the irrefutable facts.

BREAKDOWN OF THE FACTS

#1. Extremely Reliable Sources

1. The accident occurred in Arkdale, Wisconsin. The story, including the community's response and outreach, made the Front Page of the *Wisconsin Rapids Daily Tribune* on February 5, 2007. On November 13, 2008, the paper featured a follow up story on Bruce's near-death experience and healing. The timeline of the accident is as follows:

   • Accident occurred at 18:15 on November 16, 2006

   • 911 called at 18:19

   • Med Flight arrived at the University of Wisconsin Hospital at 19:47

   • In surgery at 20:50

2. Bruce Van Natta was a successful, self-employed diesel truck mechanic with wife, Lori, and their four

children—a thirteen-year-old daughter, twelve-year-old twin boys, and a ten-year-old daughter. When I was interviewing him, like with Marolyn Ford and David Yaniv, he was extremely levelheaded and down-to-earth. He had absolutely no motive to make such a story up.

3. There were a plethora of witnesses, including his wife, pastors, friends, medical and emergency personnel, and Bruce Carlson, who I personally interviewed. Also, Bruce's community raised thousands of dollars to help cover the medical expenses.

4. The experience resulted in a complete life change and direction. Bruce closed his profitable mechanic business and is now in full-time ministry, dedicated to spreading the Gospel and leading believers into more intimate relationships with Christ. It is extremely unlikely that he would have closed down a successful business and pursued full-time ministry based on a fabricated story.

5. The undeniable medical records which confirm the miracle.

#2. Breakdown of the Medical Records

Upon request, Bruce readily supplied me with the five-page *Trauma Operative Note* from the University of Wisconsin Hospital in Madison, signed by Attending Surgeon: Michael Schurr, MD, and dated November 22, 2006. Bruce also forwarded me e-mail correspondence from the senior radiologist. He didn't attempt to manipulate anything in the report and gave me total freedom to seek other medical professionals to read through it if I so wished. I did exactly that. I took the records to Sharon Fellner, who has a Master's Degree in Genetics, taught Anatomy and Physiology at a local university, and is currently in Medical School specializing in Internal Medicine. What she uncovered in the report made the miracle even more astounding. Below are quotes taken directly from the *Trauma Operative Note,* followed by comments based on my interview with Sharon.

> Quote (A): "Small bowel resection x 3…Last night he underwent resection of the 4th portion of his duodenum and resection of mid-jejunum to terminal ileum. In all, he had 75 cm of proximal jejunum and 25 cm of distal ileum with preservation of his ileocecal valve."

The term *resection* means the surgical removal of an organ. Three portions of the small bowel were surgically removed. According to the above statement, a portion of his duodenum was removed. All of his jejunum was removed except 75 centimeters. The whole jejunum is about 250 centimeters or about 8 feet. All of his ileum was removed except 25 centimeters. The whole ileum is about 400 centimeters or about 13 feet. At this point, Bruce had 100 centimeters of small intestines left, 3.2 feet out of 21 feet. About 18 feet was resected or surgically removed.

> Quote (B): "These 3 segments were transected using GIA. These small bowels were sent for gross and permanent pathology."

GIA, the process of gastrointestinal anastomosis, is the removing of the intestine and the clamping or stapling together of the ends of the viable pieces. This statement is incredibly important because what it says is that the surgically removed small intestines were actually sent to permanent pathology. When this happens, those organs never go back into the patient. I want to stress that 18 feet of Bruce's small intestines were physically removed. They were not folded or hidden somewhere in his body.

> Quote (C): "At this point, we found approximately 75 cm of viable jejunum…Approximately 25 cm of viable but congested ileum…"

The word *viable* here means "usable." The inference of course would be that if only 100 centimeters is viable, then 550 centimeters or 18 feet is not viable. That's why they were removed.

Quote (D): "At this point were performed intraoperative Doppler examination. Proximal jejunum approximately 75 cm in length had triphasic Doppler signals…Distal portion of the distal ileum approximately 25 cm in length had also a dopplable signal but seemed congested due to decreased venous drainage."

This perhaps is the most telling quote. The Doppler exam is basically an ultrasound. This was done after the surgical removal of the small intestines. So that means the signal is only going to pick up what is actually present. If there would have been more intestines, say 300 centimeters, the Doppler would have picked it up. The fact that it only picked up 75 centimeters and 25 centimeters is because that's all that was there.

After reading over the reports, it is very clear that Bruce Van Natta had approximately 18 feet of his small intestines surgically removed, leaving him only 100 centimeters or 3.2 feet. Then, during the fourth surgery, another 5 centimeter piece was removed, leaving him with 95 centimeters. Four different times, Bruce was operated on, and in each of those surgeries, they worked on the small intestines. If there would have been more than 100 centimeters, they would have noted it. They didn't note it because they had been removed. Below are the surgery dates and descriptions.

- November 16, 2006: Date of injury and first surgery— repaired blood vessels and removed all but a little over 100 centimeters of the small intestine (leaving a small portion of the duodenum, 75 centimeters of jejunum, and 25 centimeters of the ileum left). (Documented 75 centimeters and 25 centimeters.)

- November 17, 2006: Second surgery—*finished repair and reconstruction of the intestines.* They were unable to close the abdomen completely due to swelling. (Documented 75 centimeters and 25 centimeters.)

- November 21, 2006: Third surgery—put in a feeding tube and closed abdomen. *Second part of the duodenum and the jejunum were anastamosed,* meaning they were connected together. (Documented 75 centimeters and 25 centimeters.)

- February 5, 2007: Fourth surgery—*had to cut out another 5 centimeters of intestine* due to a constricture or blockage caused by the squeezing off of the opening. (Documented now 95 centimeters.)

- June 18, 2007—small bowel X-ray showed an increase in intestinal length.

After the prayer and the new Upper G.I. exam, the senior radiologist wrote the following e-mail to Bruce:

> …As I look at the small bowel remaining, I think you have about one half of the normal length remaining. If the small bowel is thought to be anywhere from 16 to 22 feet, I am going to make the conversion into cm's easier by estimating some things. As we discussed if approximately half of the small bowel could be 9 feet, and there are approximately 3 feet to a meter (a meter is really 39 inches, not 36) then the amount of small bowel in cm's is about 300 cm's. —Dr. A.T., Senior Radiologist

Three hundred centimeters is actually closer to 10 feet, but you get the picture. If Bruce clearly only had 95 centimeters or 3 feet at the time of BC's prayer, where did the extra 205 centimeters of intestines come from? The only conclusion is that they came from God when Bruce felt a snake uncoil in his stomach. It's another medical fact that the small intestines do not regenerate.

#3. Other Important Facts that Can't Be Ignored

Bruce was wasting away, yet after prayer that day, he began to gain weight. Today he is a healthy 175 pounds. His weight level stopped dropping the day he was prayed for, he felt the electricity go through his body, and then he felt the snake uncoil in his stomach. He was dying because of lack of intestines, and now he's perfectly healthy. It all changed after prayer. A coincidence? Not hardly.

I asked Bruce, "Is there any way the doctors could have made a mistake, like you could have had that much intestines and them not know it?"

"No for a couple reasons," he said. "First of all, I wouldn't have been starving to death and wouldn't have been losing weight if I had the 10 feet of intestines. Second, there were multiple doctors on the team when they cut me open. The head doctor is the Chief Trauma Surgeon. He is renowned. He's at the top of his field. When the President of the United States came to Wisconsin, he was put on call in case something happened. So, for him to be inside of me four times, if there was some discrepancy, he would have caught it. Third, I went back in for a fifth operation. They had to remove my gall bladder because of being fed intravenously for so long. While in there, the nurses and doctors saw all the extra intestines that were not there before."

"Why didn't God give you back all twenty-one feet?" I asked him.

"All I know is Bruce Carlson prayed for my small intestines to grow. My stomach muscles are gone. I have like a net. When I eat, my stomach goes out. When I poop my stomach goes back in. If I were to have all my intestines, I would have a crazy amount of hernias. But, with half the amount of intestines, I'm fine. They did blood tests to see how my intestines are working, and from my blood tests, there is only one number that is not absolutely perfect, and it's a liver function. No affect on me. The G.I. specialist told me, 'the amount of intestines you have work just as well nutritionally as if you have all your intestines.' God gave me back half my intestines, but they work better than normal for my condition. 'You'll be able to live a normal life with this amount of intestines you have here,' the senior radiologist told me that day."

I interviewed both Bruce Carlson and Bruce Van Natta, and their stories matched perfectly. BC related to me how Bruce reacted when he felt the electricity go through his body and how he said, "It felt like a snake just uncoiled in my stomach."

After honestly examining all of the facts, the bottom line is that one can only conclude that Bruce Van Natta's small intestines grew out supernaturally after specific prayer.

CONCLUSION

To continue to disbelieve in miracles, or the God of miracles, is to simply refuse to acknowledge the facts. It is a sheer resolve of the will, not wanting to believe. The truth is, miracles don't usually happen, but sometimes they do. For me, I find great comfort knowing the God of miracles is involved in my life, whether I receive a miracle or not. If I don't receive a miracle now, God has a reason, and even though I don't always understand His ways, I will eventually get my miracle in the next life. To learn more about Marolyn Ford, David Yaniv, and Bruce Van Natta see the "People Behind the Stories" section at the end of this book.

> ..."If only I may touch His clothes, I shall be made well." Immediately the fountain of her blood was dried up, and she **felt** in her body that she was healed of the affliction. And Jesus, immediately knowing in Himself that **power** had gone out of Him... (Mark 5:28-30).

Chapter 5

THE ENEMY IS REAL, REALLY REAL

There are two equal and opposite errors into which our race can fall about devils. One is to disbelieve in their existence. The other is to believe and to feel an excessive and unhealthy interest in them. —C.S. Lewis, Oxford Professor, scholar, atheist turned believer[1]

In 2009, the Barna Group published the findings from a survey of 1,871 professing Christians pertaining to the statement: "Satan is not a living being but is a symbol of evil." The results were staggering. Only twenty-six percent disagreed with the statement.[2] Not only have Hollywood and the humanistic educational system succeeded in tainting our view of Christians and their intelligence, but western secular society as a whole has so influenced the Church that much of Christendom no longer actually believes in, understands, or sees the relevance of spiritual warfare. Satan and his demonic systems are relegated to myths, novels, movies, cartoon characters, and sports mascots. Even worse, the intellectual community has labeled Satan as a folkloric philosophical metaphor for evil.

Robert M. Price, Professor of Biblical Criticism at the Center for Inquiry Institute and self-proclaimed heretic, confirms this sentiment.

The burden of my discussion here is to show you how the Satan figure evolved. We can trace the gradual, folk-loric accumulation of originally distinct elements and motifs, just like tracing, for instance, the growth of Santa Claus. That kind of tells you that the end result, whatever it is, cannot be historical fact.[3]

His argument sounds impressive, very intellectual. I think this is how the enemy would want it. In his book, *I Never Thought I'd See the Day,* Dr. David Jeremiah wrote the following:

> When I hear individuals who profess to be Christians express disbelief in the reality of Satan and demons, I wonder about the source of their beliefs. The Bible could not be more clear about the existence of the devil and the reality of the spiritual conflict going on all around us…Satan's war against us is organized and complete with strategies…Like a military general, Satan plans his attacks and directs his demonic forces. So, the more unsuspecting or unbelieving a person is concerning the reality of spiritual warfare, the more easily he or she becomes prey.[4]

In staying with the theme of this book, I must admit that, had it not been for my own personal experiences and tenacity for the facts, I too would have probably doubted the reality of Satan and demons. Actually, at one time I did struggle with the concept of a literal Satan and his kingdom of cronies, but not anymore.

THIS THING IS REAL, REALLY REAL!

I have debated long and hard about whether or not to include the following personal account in this book because I know that, in doing so, I am setting myself up for ridicule. Certainly, a percentage of those who read it will conclude, along with those like Professor Price from the previous page, Richard Dawkins, and secular society, that I am most definitely delusional. So be it. For me to deny my experience would be a sheer refusal to accept reality. Like Marolyn Ford's incredible healing of blindness, if what happened to me was indeed real, then it has serious implications for how we view the world and how we live.

Remember back in Chapter 1 when I spoke of having an "out-of-the-box, supernatural incident" that helped me maintain my faith despite being ripped by my college professor? Here's what happened. Shortly after my conversion to Christianity, long on zeal and short on wisdom, I decided to read up on Satanism and the occult. There had been some occult activity in the area directed against Christianity. I told myself that I was researching to better understand what we were up against, but *curious* was probably a more accurate description. I visited the city library and checked out about a dozen or so books on Satanism, witchcraft, and the occult. Later, back at home in my bedroom, I began thumbing through the volumes, intrigued and soaking in the information. Sometime in the early afternoon, tired of reading, I closed the books and crashed on the bed for a little nap.

As I lay there that afternoon, drifting in and out of sleep, I heard what sounded like a high-pitched hum coming from the corner of my ceiling. It was strange because I had never heard it before. When I turned my head to see what the noise was, an invisible force took hold of me, jumped on my chest, and began to strangle me. I can't tell you if I was awake or asleep, but I thrashed about on the bed, literally wrestling with this unseen force. I felt helpless and thought I was going to suffocate to death. At that point, it occurred to me that the only one who could save me was Jesus. I attempted to scream His name, but the invisible force had seized my mouth as well. Whatever it was, it desperately wanted to keep me from saying the name of Jesus. Finally, with slurred and twisted speech, the word "Jesus!" burst forth from my mouth. Instantly, the force departed. I sat up in bed, drenched in sweat, completely drained of energy.

Physically and emotionally shaken, not knowing what had just happened, I picked up the phone and called the lady I refer to as my "spiritual mom." Without giving details, I told her to get to my house as quickly as possible. Sensing the desperation in my voice, she dropped what she was doing and rushed over. Roughly thirty minutes later, she arrived at my house, along with one of the pastors from our church. After I described to them what had happened, the pastor observed the books on my floor, shook his head, and said, "When you read these books, you opened your mind up to demonic activity, and a demon jumped on you." We prayed through the house, and they took the books away. For days afterward, I walked around in a daze, mumbling over and over, "*It's real. It's real. This thing is really real.*" Though I was a Christian, I had not been completely convinced of the demonic realm. Now, my eyes had been opened.

What happened to me was not imagined. I am not exaggerating or lying, nor am I writing about it to be sensational. It really *did* happen. Over the years, I've examined this event from every possible angle. I've researched sleep disorders such a narcolepsy and sleep paralysis. They were ruled out. I'm also familiar with REM sleep. This is a stage during sleep when Rapid Eye Movement occurs. During REM sleep, the large voluntary muscles of the body are paralyzed. Conversely, brain activity is quite intense at this stage. It is during REM sleep that most of our extreme dreams occur. I've talked to doctors and experts, and after careful analysis of the facts, my conclusion is that it *was* a demon spirit.

Think about it. This intense experience just happened to occur only minutes after soaking my mind for hours with satanic material. The presence of evil was so strong that I knew only Jesus could defeat it. That's why I called out His name. If it was narcolepsy or sleep paralysis, why had I never before experienced a single incident—not once in my entire life? In addition, all of this went on in the middle of the afternoon, not at night, and, I stress again, only minutes after polluting my mind with satanic material. The incident was so disturbing to me that I immediately called someone to rush over. Why would I, a confident, athletic young man, do such a thing if it was only a bad dream? I'd had dozens of bad dreams before. This wasn't one. It was much more. Believe what you want.

All I can say is that it *actually* happened and was not the result of an overactive imagination. Nor was it some sleep disorder. Is it intellectual for me to talk about it? Nope. Will unbelievers and even some believers mock me? Yep. But to deny what happened would be a lie and unethical to you and myself.

JESUS CERTAINLY BELIEVED IN SATAN AND DEMONS

Jesus walked in the understanding that Satan and demons are real. He never questioned their reality and even proclaimed Satan as *"the ruler of this world"* (John 14:30). On another occasion, Jesus said, *"…Away with you, Satan! For it is written, 'You shall worship the Lord your God, and Him only you shall serve"* (Matt. 4:10). If Jesus is the Son of God, God incarnate, then we must embrace all of what He said. I'm sure you've heard the old Lord, Liar, or Lunatic argument. Jesus was one of the three. He was not just some great moral teacher, as some would suggest. If Jesus was not God, as He declared to be, then He was in fact a liar or lunatic. But *if* Jesus was God in the flesh, then it behooves us to follow all of His teachings because His words are truth. Jesus referred to Satan twenty-five times and had personal encounters with him. Someone has calculated that twenty-five percent of Jesus' actions, parables, and miracles had to do with demons. Jesus clearly thought that demons were real.[5]

The apostle Paul followed in Jesus' steps when he said,

> *Put on the whole armor of God, that you may be able to stand against the wiles of the devil. For we do not wrestle against flesh and blood, but against principalities, against powers, against the rulers of the darkness of this age, against spiritual hosts of wickedness in heavenly places"* (Ephesians 6:11-12).

On another occasion, Paul said, *"…[beware] lest Satan should take advantage of us; for we are not ignorant of his devices"* (2 Cor. 2:11). It's hard to understand Satan's devices if we don't believe he exists! The New Testament writers consistently acknowledged a literal, spiritual opposition that is present in the world and that we are at war against.

Harvard-educated psychiatrist and mega-bestselling author M. Scott Peck, MD, used to question the reality of Satan. In his book, *People of The Lie: The Hope for Healing Human Evil,* he wrote the following:

> I was left facing an obvious intellectual question: Is there such thing as evil spirit? Namely, the devil? I thought not. In common with 99 percent of psychiatrists and the majority of clergy, I did not think the devil existed. Still, priding myself on being an open-minded scientist, I felt I had to examine the evidence that might challenge my inclination in the matter...I now know Satan is real. I have met it...Conversion to a belief in God generally requires some kind of actual encounter—a personal experience—with the living God. Conversion to a belief in Satan is no different...Before witnessing my first exorcism, and while I was intrigued, I was hardly convinced of the devil's reality. It was another matter after I had personally met Satan face-to-face. There is no way I can translate my experience into your experience. It is my intent, however, that, as a result of my experience, closed-minded readers will become more open-minded in relation to the reality of evil spirit...Moreover, obscure though it might be, I do believe there is some relationship between Satanic activity and human evil.[6]

TWO HIGHLY EDUCATED, THEOLOGICALLY-BALANCED PASTORS ENCOUNTER DEMONS

Chip Ingram is a successful pastor and a graduate of Dallas Theological Seminary, a seminary highly respected by many denominations that emphasizes intellectual knowledge of the Bible rather than subjective experience. Listen to Chip's personal account:

I was lying in bed, half awake and half asleep. It started out like a bad dream, but suddenly there was a foreboding evil presence in the room. There was intense pressure on my chest that felt like a five-thousand-pound weight crushing me and a tightness around my neck that completely closed my windpipe. I was paralyzed; I couldn't move any part of my body except my eyes. I was desperate for air like someone under water who can't get to the surface fast enough. My thoughts were racing: "Oh, God, help me, help me, Jesus, help…." I could see my wife asleep next to me, and I just kept praying and praying, clueless as to what was going on and wondering how in the world someone could suffocate in his own bed. And then the pressure suddenly left. I gasped for air, I could move again, and I sat up in bed, coughing, my body as soaked with perspiration as if I had played basketball for two hours. The hair on the back of my neck was sticking straight up, and there was a sense of manifest evil in the room that I had never felt in my life. I was scared to death. It was hostile, demonic activity…That was in Santa Cruz, California, a community in which occult activity thrives, and it happened shortly after I had moved there to pastor the Santa Cruz Bible Church.[7]

What an eye-opening account. Chip Ingram was convinced! Yet, for those die-hard skeptics who are still holding onto the sleep paralysis thing, please reserve your final judgment until after this next story.

At the time of this writing, Ross Purdy is the lead pastor of Burbank Presbyterian Church in Burbank, California. In 2000, he was the pastor of Lake Arrowhead Community Presbyterian Church in Lake Arrowhead, California. Ross is a graduate of Princeton Theological Seminary and California State University, Fullerton. He is highly educated and part of a moderate, balanced, denomination that is typically reserved when it comes to modern supernatural experiences. Ross has no reason to fabricate a story like the one below. There is absolutely nothing for him to gain. He shares his story for one reason. It is true.

One afternoon in February of 2000, Ross and a pastor friend named Dale visited a couple's home who had reported strange paranormal activity going on—like tableware moving involuntarily on a counter top for several feet before their very eyes and their three-year-old son carrying on conversations with shadows in the corners that even involved him answering questions. The non-Christian couple had contacted Ross because they were concerned for their son's safety and knew nowhere else to turn. Though Ross did believe in demonic activity, casting out evil spirits wasn't part of his regular job description. Because he knew that any demon spirit was subject to Christ's authority, Ross' primary concern was leading the couple to Christ. The first thing the two pastors did when they arrived was explain the Gospel. The couple was receptive and prayed to receive Christ.

Next, Ross, Dale, and the couple walked through the house, room by room, praying over it. When they came to the stairway that led to the basement, where the boy frequently played, Ross and Dale proceeded down. The couple, however, stayed upstairs. While walking down the stairs, Ross felt a sudden burst of cold air, as if someone had opened a refrigerator door. Though he thought it was strange, Ross stayed calm and level-headed, continuing to pray. Once in the basement, Ross and Dale paced the floor praying. Here's what happened next. It's from the book, *Encountering Heaven and the Afterlife: True Stories from People Who Have Glimpsed the World Beyond.*

> Dale stepped into a laundry room around the corner from the stairs. Ross wandered around…Soon he walked back to meet Dale. As Ross turned the corner, he was stunned. Dale had stepped out of the laundry room and was crouched down with his back against the

wall. He was huddled in an almost fetal position, and his face wore an expression of pain and fear.

Ross hurried toward him. "Dale, what happened? Are you okay?"

Dale stayed near the floor, silent, trembling. Finally he said in a near whisper, "I'm okay. Just give me a few minutes."

Ross couldn't help but notice how visibly shaken Dale appeared. "I'm going to keep praying—for this house and also for you."

…[Ross] felt a strong impression that he should pray while walking up the stairway. Halfway up…still praying for Dale and against any evil in the house, suddenly an unseen force shoved him back against the wall. *Wham!* It was as if an invisible wrestler had body-slammed him. Up against the wall, he felt a large pair of hands choking his throat. Ross continued praying—more frantically and now silently since he could not speak or breathe.

Heavenly Father, help me. I rebuke this evil in the name of Jesus Christ! Immediately, the pressure ceased from around his neck, and he gulped in air.

With adrenaline coursing through his body, Ross sensed something moving, something he couldn't see. Though he couldn't visibly detect it, he had no doubt something was there. He followed the being or entity as it entered the dark storage area. It was as if this evil thing had retreated to its shadowy hole for safety. Still praying, Ross asked Jesus to remove all evil [and the evil spirit left].[8]

Another eye opened. Ross Purdy is convinced! One of the things I want to point out about Ross' story is that many of the manifestations he experienced were the same as the ones Chip Ingram and I experienced—smothering, pressure, choking, struggling to speak. Yet for Ross, it all occurred while he was wide awake, walking up a staircase! Again, I want to point out that Ross is a successful pastor in a very moderate denomination. He's a graduate of Princeton, not Bob's Bible Academy. He has nothing to gain by such a story. For anyone to deny that it actually happened would be a blatant refusal to accept the facts. As I said before, my reason for sharing these stories is not to sensationalize, but to show how real the spiritual world and spiritual warfare are.

So what do we do with all this information? First, we must wake up and realize there is an actual spiritual battle going on for our souls and the souls of our loved ones! Too many of us claim to be believers, but live as if we are atheists. We go through the motions of our church rituals and can speak the religious lingo, but our hearts are far from Him. We're so distracted by our cell phones, computers, and televisions that our relationship with God gets put on the back burner. The truth is, if Satan can use his system to distract us or get us to *not* believe, then he has won.

It's important to point out that we as believers have nothing to fear. God's Spirit resides in us. Nor are we to be overly demon conscious. Satan typically works through philosophies of vain deceit and world systems. Most of our temptations come from our own fleshly desires. Satan uses his devices to distort, pervert, and inflame those desires. This is not a "blame all my problems on the devil" chapter. I shared this chapter to show you the reality of the spiritual wickedness in high places and the sanity of belief in them. Our job as Christ-followers is to be alert and sober-minded, to simply do what God's Word tells us to do.

> *Be sober, be vigilant; because your adversary the devil walks about like a roaring lion, seeking whom he may devour. Resist him, steadfast in the faith…* (1 Peter 5:8-9).

> *Finally, my brethren, be strong in the Lord and in the power of His might. Put on the whole armor of God, that you may be able to stand against the wiles of the devil. For we do not*

wrestle against flesh and blood, but against principalities, against powers, against the rulers of the darkness of this age, against spiritual hosts of wickedness in the heavenly places (Ephesians 6:10-12). [Verses 12-18 explain what the armor of God consist of.]

But even if our gospel is veiled, it is veiled to those who are perishing, whose minds **the god of this age** *has blinded, who do not believe, lest the light of the gospel of the glory of Christ, who is the image of God, should shine on them* (2 Corinthians 4:3-4).

Chapter 6

HEARING GOD'S VOICE OR JUST HEARING VOICES?

Nothing in this world compares to hearing God's voice.
—Charles F. Stanley[1]

Thus far in this book, we've established, by the observation of some undeniable facts, that it is quite *sane* to believe in the existence of God, in miracles, and in a very real spiritual realm where demonic and angelic activity is occurring. But to believe that God actually speaks to us personally and gives specific directions concerning the details of our lives may sound to some as the epitome of *insanity,* especially our atheist and agnostic friends. When anyone claims to hear from God, the committed unbeliever frequently pulls out the ole' "they're delusional" card and points to people like serial killer Peter William Sutcliffe, known as "The Yorkshire Ripper." Sutcliffe was convicted of murdering thirteen women and attacking seven others in the United Kingdom. After he was arrested, he told police that God had given him detailed instructions to murder the women. The basis of his defense strategy was the claim that he was a tool of God's will. Somehow, I don't think that's the same voice that Charles Stanley was suggesting in the above quote.

While penning this chapter, I happened to see on the news that authorities had apprehended a stalker of actress Selena Gomez. Upon cross-examination, the stalker claimed to have had over fifty conversations a day with God and that God had told him that he and Selena were supposed to be a couple and bear children. The problem was (sarcasm intended), God didn't let Selena in on the "divine plan."

When considering examples such as the ones above, I must admit, the atheists do have a point. Philippe Huguelet, MD, and Sylvia Mohr, PhD, concluded from their ongoing study of delusional patients that many of those who believed they had an intimate relationship with God also believed that God instructed them to inflict serious bodily injury to themselves or to others. They found that these same patients often heard God's voice telling them to pray, go to church, read their Bible, and not to take medication because it would hinder their ability to hear God's voice.[2]

In the case of religious cults, almost one hundred percent of the time, they are founded by leaders who claim to have heard God speak directly to them and impart "special" revelation that only they possess. Typically, their so-called "special" revelations are used to control their followers under the guise of religion. The Heaven's Gate cult is a prime example. Thirty-nine of its members committed mass suicide on March 26, 1997. They did so because they believed that God had spoken directly to their leader Marshall Applewhite and given him "special" revelation about the end of the world. Applewhite also declared that he was the individual whose mind was the reincarnation of Jesus Christ. What he probably never told his followers was that, back in 1972, he was committed to a Houston psychiatric hospital because of severe depression and hearing voices.

I can't tell you how many times I've heard believers claim that God spoke to them when making statements or plans, only for the end results to be erroneous, making the believer and Christianity appear ludicrous. I have a minister friend who was highly successful in the ministry at a young age. He was good-looking, charismatic, kind-hearted, and single until his early thirties. In the eyes of many single Christian women, he was the perfect catch. On more than one occasion down through the years, he was approached by sincere Christian women who were certain God had spoken to them that he was "the one" they were supposed to marry. His response was usually something like, "When God tells me, you'll be the first to know." Eventually, God brought the right woman into his life at the right time, and they've made a great ministry team.

I too am guilty, especially in my younger, more zealous years, of claiming God had spoken to *me,* only for it sometimes to turn out to be my own will or emotions speaking. I think it's safe to conclude that many irrational, unhealthy, religious, and even sincere Christian people hear voices that they *think* are from God. So here's the question. Despite the schizophrenia, despite all the times believers misinterpret inner promptings that they think are God, and despite all the whackos getting "special" revelations, does God actually speak to us personally?

Just as they do with the subject of miracles, the radical atheists and ultra-skeptics tend to sweep everyone who believes God speaks into the "delusional" category. In addition, some Christians hold to certain rigid doctrinal positions that claim God doesn't speak personally any longer and signs and wonders ceased with the apostles or the canonization of the New Testament.[3] For them, extra-biblical experiences and encounters with God are frowned upon, often heckled at, and even attributed to Satan. I heard one puffed-up theologian say, "Any signs and wonders done today are 'false' and straight from Satan and are deceiving people."

Now, I certainly understand that Satan can and does do false signs and wonders, but only because he seeks to counterfeit the real things that God is doing. Discerning believers with the Holy Spirit residing inside them should be able to tell the difference. I fear for the preachers and theologians who attribute things that God is doing to Satan. I'd like for those who don't believe that God does true signs and wonders or speaks today to have conversations with Marolyn Ford, David Yaniv, or Bruce Van Natta. In all three stories, if someone hadn't heard from God and obeyed, Marolyn would have likely remained blind, David would have likely remained paralyzed, and Bruce would quite possibly be dead! While believers in Christ cannot compromise the fundamental tenets of our faith, some of us need deliverance from doctrinal ignorance and arrogance! God can and often does step outside of our human-made, religious boxes to accomplish His purposes.

After hearing God speak very specifically into my own life and into the lives of others, and journalistically reviewing the facts of those encounters, I can confidently answer the question of "Does God speak personally?" with "Most definitely, yes!" Not only does God still speak to us, but He wants to speak directly to us on an intimate level. Yet, as Charles Stanley says, "If we come to Him doubting His ability to speak, we will have a difficult time listening. So we must come expectantly."[4] Other respected leaders agree. Here are some of their quotes:

> God will speak to the hearts of those who prepare themselves to hear... —A.W. Tozer[5]

> If you want to hear God's voice clearly and you are uncertain, then remain in His presence until He changes this uncertainty. —Corrie Ten Boom[6]

> I do not make a major decision, especially one involving others, without a specific word from my Shepherd. —Anne Graham Lotz[7]

> We fail to hear God's voice (in Scripture and through others and through the direct impressions put upon us by His Holy Spirit) and see His hand of providence in dozens of things that come our way throughout the day, and thousands throughout our lives...So we need to become more alert to seeking and hearing God's voice. —Randy Alcorn[8]

Does God really speak to His people in our day? Yes! Will He reveal to you where He is working when He wants to use you? Yes! God has not changed. He still speaks to His people. If you have trouble hearing God speak, you are in trouble at the very heart of your Christian experience. —Henry Blackaby[9]

Yes, God definitely speaks to His children. The latter part of this chapter is dedicated to modern-day accounts of God speaking personally and specifically to people with supernatural results, and I use that word *supernatural* with the utmost respect and care. Before we delve into their stories, however, there are some quick guidelines to follow in hearing God's voice. Sticking to them should keep us from going off course.

SOME GUIDELINES FOR SAFELY DISCERNING GOD'S VOICE

#1. All true believers have the Holy Spirit residing within them.

The Holy Spirit speaks and guides the true believer. *"You are the temple of God and...the Spirit of God dwells in you"* (1 Cor. 3:16). The Holy Spirit resides inside believers; therefore, He can speak clearly and distinctly at any time, in any way He wishes.

> *And I will pray the Father, and He will give you another Helper, that He may abide with you forever—the Spirit of truth, whom the world cannot receive, because it neither sees Him nor knows Him; but you know Him, **for He dwells with you and will be in you*** (John 14:16-17).

The following are a few biblical examples of the Holy Spirit speaking directly.

As they ministered to the Lord and fasted, the **Holy Spirit said**, "Now separate to Me Barnabas and Saul for the work to which I have called them" (Acts 13:2).

...**the Spirit said** to him, Behold [Peter], three men are seeking you (Acts 10:19).

And now, **compelled by the Sprit**, I am going to Jerusalem, not knowing what will happen to me there. I only know that in every city **the Holy Spirit warns me** that prison and hardships are facing me (Acts 20:22-23 NIV).

...they were **forbidden by the Holy Spirit** to preach the word in Asia. After they had come to Mysia, they tried to go into Bithynia, but **the Spirit did not permit them** (Acts 16:6-7).

The Spirit told Philip, "Go to that chariot and stay near it" (Acts 8:29 NIV).

#2. God speaks primarily through His Word, the Bible, and He will not violate it.

Scripture is the final authority. If you have an inner prompting that doesn't line up with a proper understanding of God's Word, then it's not from God, period, regardless of your experience. There are no "special" revelations that violate or are above God's written Word. Here's a simple example. You may "feel" like it's the right thing to have an affair on your spouse because this other person is meeting some need of yours, or you may "feel" there are many different paths to God outside of Jesus Christ—but those feelings are not from God because the Scriptures are plain on these issues. You are being influenced by a spirit, just not the Holy Spirit. In the next chapter, we will get into the overwhelming evidence for the authority of the Bible.

#3. Learning to hear God's voice comes through relationship.

When my wife calls me on the phone, I instantly know it's her. How? After spending years with her, recognizing her voice is second nature. The more time we spend with God and get to know Him, the easier it becomes to sense the Holy Spirit prompting us. Most of the time, it's a quiet, peaceful knowing deep in our spirits. Jesus said, *"My sheep hear My voice, and I know them, and they follow me"* (John 10:27). A mature relationship with God, however, is not like the ones in the delusional study. Those people clearly step outside the system of checks and balances that God Himself has set up, and some are affected by mental illness.

#4. Satan speaks, and our own wills and emotions speak.

For everything God has, Satan has a counterfeit. Also, our own wills and emotions can be pretty convincing at times. Hearing God, therefore, becomes a matter of discernment. This discernment can be developed and honed. With the Holy Spirit in you and the Bible as your compass, you will be able to discern the different voices in your life. Some require action; some are borne out over time.

> *But the natural man does not receive the things of the Spirit of God, for they are foolishness to him; nor can he know them, because they are **spiritually discerned*** (1 Corinthians 2:14).

#5. God will confirm His voice through other people.

Each believer in the body of Christ is called to be in relationship with others. We need other believers who can offer balanced counsel, truth, and discernment to us. Whenever we become isolated, we fall into the danger of becoming unbalanced. This is why the Scripture urges us to *"not* [forsaking] *the assembling of ourselves together"* (Heb. 10:25). Also, God has provided in the church body those individuals with gifts that can help us discern.

> *And He Himself gave some to be apostles, some prophets, some evangelists, and some pastors and teachers, for the equipping of the saints for the work of ministry, for the edifying of the body of Christ...that we should no longer be children tossed to and fro and carried about with every wind of doctrine...* (Ephesians 4:11-14).

People with different gifts in the Church are to protect us from getting off track. For me personally, God has used my wife as a guide. Almost always, if what I'm feeling is of God, she will have a peace about it and be in agreement with me. If not, it's usually not of God. Also, God has consistently put godly men in my life as friends to speak truth to me. They have the authority to speak to me because we are in relationship and they know me personally. I value these relationships like gold. Always be careful who you listen to, however. Just because someone is behind a pulpit or in a church doesn't mean that person is speaking truth or has the authority to speak into your life. Discernment is needed here as well. Still, if something is from God, God will confirm it through other people, and you will know it.

#6. God confirms His voice through circumstances.

Another way God confirms His voice is through circumstances in our lives. If what you are hearing is of God, no matter how impossible it may seem, the circumstances will eventually line up. If they don't, then it was probably not God. When God is speaking, He sometimes opens and closes doors so that what He is saying becomes more evident.

> *Trust in the Lord with all your heart, and lean not on your own understanding; in all your ways acknowledge Him, and He shall **direct** your paths* (Proverbs 3:5-6).

God is in the business of directing our paths, and sometimes that's through circumstances.

#7. If it is God, you will have an abiding peace or "witness" in your spirit.

If an inner prompting is truly from God, you will experience His peace. *"But the wisdom that is from above is first pure, then peaceable, gentle..."* (James 3:17). *"...And the peace of God, which surpasses all understanding, will guard your hearts and minds through Christ Jesus"* (Phil. 4:7). God is not the author of confusion. If you are hearing from God, you will feel abiding peace in your heart. On the other hand, if something or a direction is not of God, you will feel uneasiness in your spirit as a warning.

One of the benefits of serving God for as long as I have (thirty-four years and counting) is that I can look back over the years and see what God has done in my own life. In addition, as a writer, I've had the privilege of coming in contact with others who have served God for many years, and I benefit from hearing their stories. I can assure you, with evidence from both my own life and the lives of others, that God does still speak today. The rest of this chapter is dedicated to accounts of God speaking personally in believers' lives, resulting in events that would have to be placed in the *supernatural* category. As with the miracles in Chapter 4, each account is so *powerful* and so *specific* that it is highly unlikely to be coincidence. Either the account is of God or is an outright fabrication. Each of these stories leaves little doubt that God does speak today in a very personal way.

As a journalist, I'm keenly aware of how truth can be distorted or improved upon through writing skill. These stories are written as they occurred and without embellishment. Though skeptics say testimonies and stories are notoriously unreliable, there is an undeniable power in truthful testimonies. The Christian Church owes its very existence to the power of testimonies. The apostle Paul is a prime example. Everywhere he went, he basically told his story. When defending himself from an angry mob in Jerusalem, Paul recounted his story of how he was persecuting Christians and then Jesus appeared to him on the Damascus Road (see Acts 22). He gives specific details about the event. When Paul was brought before King Agrippa, and the king said to him, "You are permitted to speak for yourself," Paul again told his Damascus Road story in detail (see Acts 26).

While we ought not be gullible and blindly accept just anything someone is saying, it is nonsensical to automatically discredit personal accounts of God moving in people's lives. We can do our homework. The more Christians share their accounts of God intervening in their lives, the more the world will see that God is real, that miracles do happen, and that prayer does work. That's why this book is filled with testimonies. Revelation 12:11 says, *"And they have overcome (conquered) him by means of the blood of the Lamb and by the utterance of their testimony…"* (AMP).

Each of the following accounts was written by respectable, well-documented believers committed to furthering the Gospel of Christ. I've also included some of my own personal accounts. The details I share in the stories are important to experience the full impact of the event in the end. These stories are not meant to imply that every time God speaks to us it will be in dramatic fashion. Most of the time, it's not dramatic at all. Finally, by sharing the following accounts, it does not mean that I necessarily endorse their doctrinal position. In each story, except for the ones that involve me personally, I give an introduction about the person and then let them tell their stories in their own words.

THE "SUPERNATURAL" WAY THIS BOOK GOT PUBLISHED BY MAX DAVIS

In 2010, my fiftieth year, I chronicled the details of my life in a daily journal. In the past, I've kept loose journals that I would write in every so often. This was the first and only time that I journaled every day for an entire year. At the time, I didn't know why I was journaling daily, but looking back, I now know. God was doing a special work in my life that year where several significant "God" things occurred that affected my life's direction. One such "God" thing concerned the publishing of this book.

I had finished writing the proposal for *The Insanity of Unbelief,* but for various reasons, it had not been published. Then, on Wednesday May 12, 2010, I felt like God spoke to my spirit about a particular publisher. After intense prayer that day, while push mowing our grass, Destiny Image Publishers came clearly to my mind, followed by deep peace. I had never published anything with Destiny Image nor, to my knowledge, did I have any contacts with them. I was, however, aware of their work and had read a couple of their books. One of their books had touched me in a significant way. It's hard to explain, but it was like I just knew in my spirit that they were supposed to be the publisher for this book. The impression had such an impact on me that I recorded it in my journal. The following is taken directly from my entry for that day.

> Have sweet spirit of peace upon me. Read Ephesians Chapter 1 & 2. Very significant…Had an hour prayer time in office. It was awesome! Power and peace like never before. I feel I'm entering a new level of relationship with God. Intersession is becoming a more foundational part of my life and success. Push mowed for 2 hours. *Destiny Image publishers keeps coming to my mind…*

Over the next month or so, Destiny Image was consistently on my mind as a good fit for this book. In my July 30th entry, I wrote, "…Destiny Image came back in my mind…I also called Karen [my agent]. She said her relationship with Destiny Image is strong…" Clearly, I was still feeling impressed about Destiny Image. Every time I thought of them, a peace and calm, a knowing, would fill my heart. Funny thing is, we never sent in the proposal, nor did my agent contact them because I got involved in another writing project that took the next eleven months. It was a project that required incredible focus and energy.

After the completion of that book in July of 2011, I traveled to have a face-to-face meeting with my agent where we mapped out the next several years of my writing career. In that meeting, I once again reminded Karen about my impressions concerning Destiny Image for *The Insanity of Unbelief*. She agreed they would be a good fit, but yet again, because of some other more "pressing" projects, we decided not to present that proposal just then and wait for the right timing.

Now, before I tell you the *supernatural* part of the story, you must understand that my agent never contacted Destiny Image Publishers on my behalf, and I had no communication or connection with them. Nada. Zero. My agent had sold a couple of books to them for other authors, but they did not know me or who represented me. And as far as I knew, they were just one of hundreds of other Christian publishers out there. Another thing that is important to note in order to get the full impact of this story is that each one of those hundreds of Christian publishers has thousands of manuscripts they are sifting through. This is not an exaggeration. The odds of even getting published are staggering. However, if God wants something done, He'll make a way, regardless of the odds. Remember, God confirms His voice through people and circumstances.

One evening my wife, Alanna, and I were walking out the door of our house to go on a date when the phone rang. It was the landline, and I have this thing about *not* answering the landline because it's almost always telemarketers. My reasoning was that anyone who knows me personally can get me on my cell. Because we rarely answer our landline, we only have minimum service—no caller I.D. or voicemail. As Alanna was stepping through the door, she reached back and picked up the phone. I rolled my eyes thinking "Why'd you do that?"

"Yes. Sure. He's right here," she said, handing me the phone. "It's for Max," she said, emphasizing *Max* because telemarketers usually asked for "Perry," which is my first name. I cautiously took the phone.

You can imagine my shock and excitement when I discovered the voice on the other end of the line was one of Destiny Image Publisher's top executives! It was someone I'd never met face-to-face, but had worked with on a project years prior when he was at another company.

"I've been trying to contact you," he said. "I've called this number several times over the past weeks and never got an answer. I was sitting here and told myself I was going to give it one more shot. I'm glad I finally got you."

He went on to tell me that for some reason he couldn't stop thinking about me and called to see if I had the rights to one of my previously published books that was now out of print. He remembered that particular book from ten years ago! I told him that I did have the rights, and then we discussed other projects that I was working on. I told him about *The Insanity of Unbelief* and how I had felt impressed they were supposed to be the publisher for it. Long story short, I e-mailed him the proposal. He loved it and forwarded it to the acquisition editor, who got so jazzed about it that I was offered a nice contract within a week. That's unheard of in the publishing business where less than one percent of manuscripts even get published.

What are the odds of Destiny Image calling me—the exact publisher that the Holy Spirit had impressed upon my heart so much so that I recorded it in my journal more than once? In my twenty-something-year career as a writer, that was the only time a publisher had ever called me out-of-the-blue like that. The process is usually the exact opposite. My agent contacts a publisher and asks them if they will review my proposal. If they say "yes," she sends it to them, and then we wait…and wait…and wait for a response. Typically, because editors are overwhelmed with proposals and manuscripts, my agent has to continue calling them over a period of weeks or months to foster a response. This time, I didn't do anything but answer my phone. Was it God? You tell me. I think God wanted this book out in His perfect timing.

YOU'RE IN THE WRONG COFFEE SHOP BY MAX DAVIS

"Your attorney is walking in a spirit of fear, the fear of a lawsuit," the voice permeated my mind as I walked around the track, crying out to God. It was about 9 p.m. "You cannot do what I called you to do walking in this fear. The fear will shut you down." The voice was crystal clear and the message even clearer. There was no mistaking it. I continued walking around the track, this time shouting out loud, "God, I've done everything honestly and legally. This is a good plan."

My partners and I had spent a year developing what we felt was a solid business plan under the wise guidance of someone extremely knowledgeable in this particular business and highly ethical. But this "revised" plan developed by our new attorney looked nothing like the original. So much had been changed that it was confusing to me. Of course, we had to protect ourselves and others involved, but this was like legal mumble jumbo, and I couldn't understand it! I felt weighed down and discouraged, and I wanted to give up.

As I continued to walk around the track, the voice spoke again, "Your attorney is walking in a spirit of fear, the fear of a lawsuit. You cannot do what I called you to do walking in this fear. The fear will shut you down."

"God," I said out loud, "I release it into Your hands. I give you this fear of a lawsuit." As soon as I said those words, it was like a thousand-pound weight lifted off my back. I flipped open my cell phone and called my partner, Don Griffin. "Don, he completely rewrote everything! I can't understand any of it! I feel like God is saying he's walking in a spirit of fear, the fear of a lawsuit. We can't do what God called us to do if we are fearful."

The next morning, I drove from my home office in the country twenty-something miles across town to sit in a coffee shop to review the new business plan and figure out what I should do because this had us stopped in our tracks. When I walked into this particular coffee shop, to my surprise, Don Griffin was sitting at a booth just waiting *as if we had a planned meeting.* First off, Baton Rouge has a population of about 300,000, including a major university, and there are over one hundred coffee shops. I sat down across from Don and immediately began pouring out my frustration about the situation. I again told him the same thing I'd told him the night before, "God says our attorney is walking in a spirit of fear of a lawsuit. We can't walk in fear and do what God called us to do."

When I finished those words, Don calmly reached into his briefcase and pulled out a computer printout. "I woke up at 2 a.m. last night," he said. "I couldn't sleep and got on my computer. When I did, I saw that someone had sent me this e-newsletter. I read it and felt I was supposed to print it out and put it in my bag. Here; read it."

I took the newsletter in my hands and began to read. Then tears began to fill my eyes as I read the sentences Don had underlined. It was a ministry newsletter from Rick Joyner. Listen to what it said:

> Increasing fear, which shuts down initiative...There is a legal mentality rooted in paranoia, an exaggerated fear of lawsuits. It has our country tied down like the fictional character, Gulliver...Why do lawyers write twenty-five pages when they could write four? The language of the lawyer, legalese, is the language of Babylon,

which means "confusion." It is a crushing weight on our government, our economy, and our people…[10]

The words described exactly how I felt, and they were exactly in line with what I had felt the Holy Spirit told me. I knew the crushing weight Rick Joyner was talking about. *And don't get me wrong; there is a need for good, godly attorneys to make sure due diligence is done and bases are covered. We need good attorneys to insure adequate representation, that our rights are not infringed upon and that we understand the law.* The attorney we were working with was really trying to help and had done some very helpful things, but just like the newsletter said, it was regulation overkill.

"Did the person who e-mailed this letter to you know that I called you last night about this?" I asked.

"Nope," replied Don. "They had no idea."

"I can't believe this, Don!" I said with tears still in my eyes. "This is exactly what God told me last night…exactly!"

Don looked at me and said, "Wait, you haven't heard the best part."

"What?"

"This morning I went to another coffee shop, CC's on Perkins Road. The parking was packed so I waited for about five minutes for an opening. Finally, someone came out of the shop, and I waited for them to get into their car and leave. Then I pulled into the spot, turned off the engine, grabbed my computer, got out of the car, locked the doors, and walked inside. When I stepped inside the door, the Holy Spirit spoke to me and said, 'You're in the wrong coffee shop.' I had a little argument in my head because I didn't want to leave the shop after going to all the trouble to get here. But the thought persisted, so I turned around and walked back to my car, got in, and left. Once on the road I said, "Okay God, where to?" and this is where I wound up. I've been here waiting for two hours. I knew God was going to send someone."

This was a divine appointment if there ever was one. Think about it. What are the odds of me walking into a random coffee shop where Don was just sitting there waiting? The night before, feeling crushed under the weight of the overregulation of the rewritten business plan, I had called Don, telling him, "God says the attorney is walking in a spirit of fear of a lawsuit and that we can't walk in fear." Then Don received the newsletter at 2 a.m. that morning, confirming what God had said. He printed it out, put it in his bag, and gave it to me when I happened to walk into the coffee shop where he was waiting after God told him he was in the wrong coffee shop before. I think it's safe to say that God was directing us! There is absolutely no way this could be mere coincidence. It's way too specific. The only explanation is that the Holy Spirit spoke to Don and me and then confirmed it.

EXCUSE ME, SIR, IS YOUR DAUGHTER IN TROUBLE? BY CHARLES STANTON

Christy Phillippe is an accomplished editor and ghostwriter with a solid reputation in the publishing world. She's received numerous awards and has worked on a number of *New York Times* bestsellers. The following account comes from a personal interview she conducted with Charles Stanton several years ago. I spoke with Christy to verify the interview and the accuracy of the information.

> I am not normally one of those people who says, "God spoke to me and told me to tell you something." But one time I had an experience I can't explain any other way. I was seated between two large businessmen on a jam-packed airplane. I pulled out my handy-dandy inflatable neck pillow and scrunched down for a little nap, but I couldn't sleep. Oddly, I thought I heard the Lord say in my spirit, *The man next to you has a daughter who is in trouble. Talk to him.*

I tried to remember if I'd eaten anything recently that hadn't been properly refrigerated. *I am making things up,* I told myself. *No way. God doesn't speak to me in this way. I'm exhausted, and I'm going to sleep right now.*

Every time I closed my eyes, I kept getting the same prompt. *The man next to you has a daughter who is in trouble. Talk to him.* The man was sophisticated and elegantly dressed. He had his glasses on, reading *The Wall Street Journal.*

I said to myself, *There is no way I'm going to interrupt this guy while he is reading his paper and say, "Excuse me, sir, is your daughter in trouble?"* I kept trying to fall asleep. It was impossible.

Okay, I reasoned silently, *if this is really God nudging me, I am going to take a chance on totally humiliating myself and ask this perfect stranger about his daughter.*

I turned to the man and said, "Excuse me, sir, is your daughter in trouble?" For an instant his face had a shocked look, as if somebody had just doused him with ice water. Then he put his head back, closed his eyes, and started to sob. He let the paper fall into his lap and took off his reading glasses. His shoulders shook and the tears ran down his face.

As soon as he could speak, he turned to me and said, "How could you possibly know that? I have a daughter who is away at college, and she is in terrible trouble. She was a virgin, and she was raped by one of her employers. Now she's pregnant."

No wonder God wouldn't let me take a nap.

"The best thing I know to do, sir," I said, "is to pray. I don't know what I can say to lighten your burden. But I know that when I don't have the words, God does."

He responded, "Let's pray."

We prayed for his daughter and his family. We prayed for the employer. We prayed for the baby. When we got off the plane, he called his wife immediately, and I overheard him say, "We need to commit our lives to God! We need to start praying for our daughter, and we need to go back to church!"

Six months later, I was speaking in southern California, and to my delight, this same man came to see me. He came up to me and said, "You have no idea how your prayers changed my daughter's life. She kept the baby—she's going to give it up for adoption—and she's going to church. My wife and I have recommitted our lives to God, and we're back at church too."

A KNOCK AT THE DOOR, AND WHERE IS THE MONEY? BY SAMUEL DOCTORIAN

The next two stories are about a wonderfully unusual and godly man named Samuel Doctorian. Samuel was born in 1930, in Beirut, Lebanon, into an Armenian family. Practically all of his extended family had been slaughtered by Turkish Muslims during the Armenian Genocide. The Turkish Muslims tried to eliminate the Armenian people because they were predominantly Christian. Most were massacred because they would not deny Christ. Others were forced from their homes and driven hundreds of miles into the Syrian Desert, where they died of hunger and thirst. Eventually, when Samuel was eight, his family found refuge in Jerusalem, but they were very poor.

God, however, had a call on Samuel's life. When he was only a teenager, he attended Bible school in Jerusalem and went on to become the Founder and Director of Bible Land Mission (BLM), located in Beirut, Lebanon. The goal of BLM is to evangelize the Middle East lands and bring revival to the body of Christ around the world. Samuel ministers in some of the hardest countries in the world: Iraq, Syria, Egypt, Jordan, and Indonesia. Because he preaches the Gospel in these countries, his life is often in danger. As a result, he has been supernaturally delivered many times. Samuel is a long-time friend of my family, and I know his daughter, Jasmine, quite well. He has told me some of his experiences personally while sitting around the fireplace at my in-laws' home. One of the things that impresses me the most about Samuel, and why I trust his stories, is because of the fruit of righteousness that is in him. I've never met a man more sold out to the cause of Christ. In addition, his wife is devoted to God, and all of his grown children are devoted ministers of the Gospel. They are primarily because of Samuel's life testimony to them.

Concerning the Christian and Missionary Alliance's Bible school in Jerusalem, where he attended as a young man, I researched the school, and it was in existence in the 1940s and '50s, and the names Samuel referenced check out perfectly. Elizabeth Moll Stalcup, PhD, wrote a book on Samuel and thoroughly investigated his claims, which included traveling to the Middle East and interviewing many of the people involved. She told me personally that all of his stories checked out and that the experience radically changed her life. The name of her book on Samuel Doctorian is *God Will Not Fail You: A Life of Miracles in the Middle East and Beyond.*[11]

A Knock at the Door

My family was so poor that my parents often struggled just to put bread on the table and to keep us in school. For many years, the only job my father could find was in a British military camp called Sarafand, many miles from home, where he worked as a tailor. The camp was near the seashore, north of Tel Aviv, a long journey from Jerusalem. Father would come home once a month bringing four Palestinian pounds, equal to about four British pounds. He would give some to the grocer, some to the baker, and some here and there paying our bills, and then he would travel back to Sarafand. For years, our family saw him only once a month.

One day when I was about ten years old, I came home from school and asked my mother for a piece of bread, but my mother told us to go out and play. We raced out, but around 7 o'clock we came home hungrier than ever. "Mother, we are hungry," we clamored, but Mother would not speak to us. She only looked sad. She washed our hands, feet, and faces and told us, "Come children, come, and go to bed now. Pray your prayers and go to sleep."

"Mother," we said, "What is the matter with you? We are hungry. We want bread!" But Mother was silent. She made us kneel and pray and then said, "Goodnight, children." Then she turned down the gaslight and went to bed.

The four of us began to cry, each looking at the others completely bewildered, with tears rolling down our cheeks. We were hungry, and Mother had put us to bed! Why was she being so cruel? What had we done that she would not feed us? Finally, we cried ourselves to sleep.

At 2 o'clock in the morning, I awoke crying. "Mother," I called.

She came close to me and whispered, "What do you want, Samuel?"

"Mother," I answered, "I cannot sleep. I want bread!"

She went and got me a cup of water. "Drink this," she said, handing it to me.

"Mother," I said, "I am not thirsty. I am hungry. I want bread." Even though the gaslight was low, I could see bright tears streaming down her face. When I saw her tears, I stopped crying, drank the water, and went back to sleep.

119

When morning dawned, we woke up famished, with tears still in our eyes.

My mother was crying, too. She said, "Children, pray. We do not have any bread, and I do not know what to do. I don't know when your father will come home next, and we have nothing to eat."

My mother did not dare tell anyone that we were hungry. She believed that we should tell only God.

We could not even think of going to school when we were so hungry, so we sat around the table, crying out to God. "Father, send us bread. Father, send us bread."

Meanwhile, unbeknownst to us, God was working a miracle. There was a sudden knock on the door. "Keep quiet, children," my mother urged. "Do not make any noise. Do not let anyone know that we are praying for bread. Only tell God about our need." She wiped the tears from her eyes and went to the door. When she opened the door, a man stepped inside bearing a basket full of bread and cheese.

"Here children," he said, "take this bread. Your Father sent it to you." I ran to the basket and tore off a big hunk of bread and stuffed it into my mouth, as only a hungry child can. I was so glad that my father had sent us bread.

Years later, I learned that my earthly father had nothing to do with that basket of food! I went to the man who had brought us the bread that day and asked him, "Sarkis, what made you come to our house that morning and give us that basket of food?"

"Samuel," he confided, "I brought that bread and cheese to take to my own family in Bethlehem. I had purchased my bus ticket and was sitting on the bus, waiting for it to leave, when a voice within me said, 'Rise. Take your basket of food to the family down in the Valley of Hinnom.'

"At first I argued with God. I said, 'No, Lord, I am already late! I must get home quickly and get back to my business.' But the voice kept saying, 'Rise, take it to that family.' I protested, 'They do not need this bread.' But the voice within me kept saying, 'Rise and go. They need this bread.'"

"I could not disobey that voice," he continued. "The driver was getting ready to start the bus, so I yelled, 'Just a minute, just a minute,' and ran down the aisle. I told the driver to let me off. He reminded me that my ticket would be useless, but I only nodded my head and climbed off. I walked down into the Valley of Hinnom, to your house, an eight-minute walk from the station. I felt rather foolish, so before I knocked on the door, I paused and put my ear to the door. I could hear hungry children crying, 'Father, send us bread!' The moment I heard you children wailing, I could wait no longer. I knocked on the door, and when your mother opened the door, I told all of you, 'Your Father sent this bread. Take it.' I gave the entire basket—everything I had bought—to you."

How wonderful is the God in whom we believe. He will not fail us! He is the God of Elijah, supplying our every need. He is a great God! I praise the Lord that I believe in a Supreme Being who is *"…able to do exceeding abundantly above all that we ask or think, according to the power that works in us"* (Eph. 3:20). *"And my God shall supply all your need according to His riches in glory by Christ Jesus"* (Phil. 4:19).

From that experience, the Lord taught me that physical hunger is bad, but spiritual hunger is worse. Millions are dying for lack of spiritual food. I want to give the living bread to those who are dying so that they can eat and live.

Where Is the Money?

When I was only sixteen years old, God opened the door for me to attend the Christian and Missionary Alliance's Bible school in Jerusalem. The only problem was, I had no money. After two weeks, the principal, Rev. Ralph Freid, called me in. "Samuel," he said, "we are very happy to have you as a student. You are eating here, studying here, sleeping here. But we must know, Samuel, what about the money? Who will pay for your fee? If you like, we can divide it—20 now, 20 in three months, 20 in three more months."

I said to the principal, "Thank you for your kind offer, Brother, but I believe I am going to bring it in all at once."

"When?" he asked.

"Give me three days," I replied, "to pray about it."

"All right," he said.

I went back to my room and knelt in prayer. "Lord," I said, "I still need 60 pounds to pay for my Bible school. Lord, I need the money. You can supply it. You will supply it."

I prayed about it for three days, but at the end of that time, I still did not have the money. Freid called me again. "Samuel, three days are over; we really need to know, who's paying for you? We are glad that you are here, and we believe you are called by God to be in this school, but what about the money? We would like to know."

I bit my lip to keep from crying because I had no answer. I begged Reverend Freid for one more day.

"Okay," he said.

I hurried back to my room and cried out to God. "Lord, I am not getting up from my knees until You give me this money. I am going to stay here until You give me Your assurance that You will provide." I continued to pray, even harder. "Lord, I believe that You can send that money right now from Heaven, right now into my hand. I believe You, Lord. You are the God of miracles, the God of impossibilities…the God of supreme power. You can do it!"

The moment I began to pray with faith, I felt that I had the money. I said, "Thank You, Lord! I have the money!" I got up from my knees and wiped the tears from my eyes. I said, "Hallelujah! I have the money! But I do not know where it is."

I began to search my pockets to see if the money was there, but it was not there. "Lord," I said, "I do not feel like asking You for the money anymore because I feel I have it. But where is it, Lord?

Please show me where it is. I believe that You have given it to me, but where is it?"

I went out of my room and began to walk back and forth in the garden. "I have the money," I said to myself, "but where is it?"

Just then our dormitory cook, Mrs. Bechar, came into the garden from Prophet Street. She had been to the market and her arms were full of bags. I went to help her carry her bags. "Samuel," she asked, "have you paid the Bible School yet?"

"No, Mrs. Bechar," I said.

"Praise the Lord!" she said, full of joy.

I was dumbfounded. "What do you mean, Sister? I said that I have not paid yet. What do you mean, 'Praise the Lord?'"

"Brother Samuel," she said, "just now, while I was walking down Prophet Street, a man in the market put money in my hand. He said it was for the little Armenian boy in the Bible school."

"Who is this man?" I asked.

"He said that he has met you before, but that you do not know him well, and he does not want you to know who he is."

"How much is it?" I asked.

"Sixty pounds," she replied. "Samuel, it is for your school fees!"

Words could not express the praise and thankfulness I felt toward my Lord. Mrs. Bechar took the money up to the principal. I did not wait for him to call me. I went right up to his office and knocked on the door.

Inside, he was counting the money. "Where did this money come from, Samuel?"

I answered, "I do not know. I prayed, and the Lord supplied it! Hallelujah!"

To this day, I do not know who gave the money, but I know that God supplied it.

He is the same God today!

He is a God of miracles!

A CHICK-FIL-A MIRACLE BY MAX DAVIS

Ron DiCianni is a world renowned Christian artist with over 10 million prints distributed worldwide. More than just paintings, however, they are anointed by the Holy Spirit. When Ron appeared on *The 700 Club* to talk about a mural he had painted of the Resurrection of Christ, the show got 4 million hits on its website. The mural is currently displayed in the *Dallas Museum of Biblical Art*. Over the years, Ron has received countless reports of people having "God" encounters while viewing his art. When you look at these examples below, you'll understand why.

Not only have Ron's paintings influenced the world, but he has sold millions of books working in collaboration with such well-known authors as Max Lucado, Jerry Jenkins, Frank Peretti, Randy Alcorn, and Joni Eareckson Tada. Ron's creative mind is exploding with potential book ideas. How we met and became partners is the result of a *supernatural divine appointment because of one man hearing God speaking to him and then obeying*. When you hear the story, I think you will agree that the odds of it happening the way it did are beyond staggering.

The story involves four people—Ron DiCianni, who lives in Temecula, California; his agent, Karen Hardin, who lives in Tulsa, Oklahoma; another Ron, Ron Checki, who lives in Baton Rouge, Louisiana; and myself, also in Baton Rouge.

On April 19, 2010, Karen Hardin contacted me saying she was the agent for artist Ron DiCianni and was interested in the two of us possibly working together on some of his book projects. At that time, Karen was not my agent, and we had not spoken for over a year. We were friends and had done some work together in the past. Karen felt strongly that Ron and I would make a good team and asked me to submit a list of my latest projects. I sent her the list, which included a book collaboration I was doing with a senior host on the QVC Network.

One month later, on May 20, Karen told me that Ron wasn't interested in working with me, primarily because he had already talked with another well-known writer who was excited about collaborating with him. That was totally understandable. There was no reason for him to consider me. Karen reiterated, however, on several occasions how strongly she felt that we should be working together. But with Ron in California, her in Tulsa, and me, a virtual unknown, in Louisiana, it would take quite an effort to get us together for a face-to-face. On the flip side, I was so busy with the QVC book and other projects that I had really moved on from considering working with Ron.

Then, after almost a month, on June 10, Karen contacted me again and asked if I could possibly talk to QVC about the network reviewing Ron DiCianni's art. My response was, "Sure. I can do that, but let me feel out the optimal time." Karen sent me Ron's promotional material to give to QVC when I felt the time was right. All during this time, she was still thinking what a good writing team Ron and I would make.

Eleven days later, on Monday, June 21, I contacted Karen to tell her I felt the time was right, that this was the week I was going to talk to QVC and give them Ron's information. I asked her to please e-mail me any final promotional material she had on Ron. Now here's where the story gets *supernatural*. Remember, Ron is in California, Karen is in Tulsa, and I'm in Baton Rouge. Also, it's important to note that Ron deals with so many people that he had forgotten my name by now. Karen had only talked to him about me one time back in April. As far as QVC went, Ron knew Karen was working on it, and one of her friends was helping her. He didn't know it was me.

On Wednesday, June 23, I had a pre-set appointment with a Christian friend of mine named Ron Checki. We meet periodically at one of the local Chick-fil-A restaurants in Baton Rouge just to fellowship. I must stress here that Ron Checki knew absolutely nothing about me helping Ron DiCianni get considered by QVC. He knew nothing about Karen Hardin wanting us to be writing partners. Ron Checki didn't even know that I knew Ron DiCianni existed. *He knew nothing, absolutely nothing.* But he did know a God who knows everything.

When I woke up that Wednesday morning, I was incredibly busy under a deadline, and I didn't want to drive halfway across town to the Chick-fil-A. I wanted to go straight to my office and work. My wife, Alanna, said, "Go. Just do it." We were supposed to meet at 7:30, and I arrived a few minutes early. Sitting in a booth, I was staring out the window when Ron Checki drove up. There was another guy with him, and when they got out of the car, the other man was holding a large leather portfolio. He didn't look too excited to be there. Neither was I.

Man, I thought to myself, *he's going to try and sell me something, or it's another aspiring writer that wants me to read his stuff.* It wasn't that I didn't want to help potential writers; it's just sometimes I get so bombarded that I can't focus on my own work. Because I was under a deadline, I was feeling some pressure.

As the two men slid in the seats across from me, the expression on the other gentleman's face conveyed that he didn't want to be there either. For a few seconds, the three of us just stared at each other awkwardly. Ron Checki spoke first. I can't recall the exact words, but it went something like this. "Max, I felt strongly in my spirit that you two guys were supposed to meet. I want to introduce you to Ron DiCianni."

I about choked on my biscuit. "You're Ron DiCianni?" I blurted. "The world-famous painter from California?"

"Yep," he said, still not too enthused.

"The Ron DiCianni?"

"That would be me."

"You're not going to believe this," I said. "I'm Max Davis! I'm the guy that is helping you get looked at by QVC this very week! I'm the writer that Karen Hardin wants you to meet and work with!" Ron Checki had not given him my name.

Sitting there, I punched in Karen's number on my cell.

"Hello," she answered.

"Karen, this is Max. You are not going to believe who I'm sitting with right this minute."

"Who?"

"Ron DiCianni!"

"No way!" She was dumbfounded. We all were.

Needless to say, Ron DiCianni and I are now partners and have developed a strong friendship. Our first project is a novel. It's a Christian fantasy, and during the writing process we were overcome by the Holy Spirit on numerous occasions. God used both Ron's unique gifts and perspective, along with my writing gifts, to put together a most unique and powerful novel. We have many more book ideas in the works.

Okay, let's look at the facts. There are approximately 300 million people in the United States. Ron DiCianni lives in Temecula, California, and the very week that I'm presenting Ron to QVC, I meet him in Chick-fil-A on Millerville Road in Baton Rouge, Louisiana, because someone obeyed a prompting in his spirit. Ron DiCianni needed a writing partner, and his agent is in Tulsa wishing and praying for us to meet. After our unexpected meeting, Ron realized that I was the one for the projects he had on his heart. On top of that, time has shown that we work well together. Our personalities and styles compliment each other. Not only are the odds astronomical that we met, but the timing was perfect. Come on, Chick-fil-A on an obscure road in Baton Rouge the exact week I'm presenting him to QVC during the weeks he was seeking a writer? It would not have worked if I had met him at another time or place like a conference or something.

How did Ron Checki know? Ron DiCianni was in Baton Rouge for a quick overnight trip to meet with an organization on a possible painting project. Ron Checki was his chauffeur to and from the airport. On the morning Ron DiCianni was flying out, Ron Checki picked him up early because he felt in his spirit that it was important that he whip by Chick-fil-A and introduce us. That's why Ron DiCianni wasn't happy about the detour. He wanted to go straight to the airport, but God had other plans.

THE GUITAR BY MAX DAVIS

While studying Journalism at the University of Mississippi, I experienced an extraordinary event that I can only conclude was the result of God speaking directly to me.

One night, during the Christmas and semester break, I began my regular prayer routine. As I prayed, something happened in my mind. Just as I had felt impressed about Destiny Image Publishers, a still small voice said, *"Give your guitar away."* At the time, I was pretty obsessed with playing the guitar and singing so this was *not* something I wanted to hear or do. As a student, I didn't have much money, and giving away a very nice guitar would mean I would be without one for the foreseeable future.

I went to bed, trying to dismiss this thought, but the more I wished it away, the stronger it became. I dozed off. When I picked up my guitar the next morning, boom, the thought came back. For days, every time I picked up my guitar, that thought nagged me. It just wouldn't leave me alone. Finally, I said, "Okay, God, You win. I'll give my guitar away." As soon as I uttered those words, a name popped into my head—Bobby Clark.[12] I was puzzled because I knew that Bobby, who attended a Bible study with me, did not play the guitar. He had at times picked mine up and fiddled with it, but he could not play.

Bobby had gone home for the semester break, which meant I would have to wait a couple of weeks to see him, but my mind was resolved. Bobby was getting the guitar. When classes resumed after the break, I called Bobby and invited him to my apartment. When he arrived, we sat on the sofa, and I said to him point blank, "Bobby, you may think I'm crazy, but God wants me to give you this guitar. Here take it." I was expecting Bobby to look at me as if I'd lost my mind, but to my surprise, tears filled his eyes. Then, right there, sitting on my blue, flower-patterned sofa, he pulled out a journal from his book bag. He told me that, over the holidays, while he was worshiping in a little church in Port Gibson, Mississippi, God had spoke to him and told him to write down the following words. As long as I live, I will never forget those words. I can quote them to this day, because I've reflected on them many times. *There is a guitar, which I, the Lord God, am going to give you. Though you do not know how to play, I will teach you to play and sing praises to Me.*

Think about it. While Bobby was away for the break, the Holy Spirit compelled him to write those words. At the same time, hundreds of miles away, the Holy Spirit was speaking to me to give *my* guitar to Bobby. Then, after he returned to school, without any knowledge of what Bobby had written in his journal, I sought him out with the specific purpose to give him my guitar! Both Bobby and I were amazed. Neither of us understood why God had done what He did, but we absolutely knew He was real and personally involved in our lives. You can call it a coincidence or whatever you want. I call it God.

A GIRL'S WATCH BY DR. DAVID YONGGI CHO

Dr. David Yonggi Cho is founder and pastor of Yoido Full Gospel Church in Seoul, Korea. When Dr. Cho began to build his church, he was living in dire poverty in a one-room hovel with a dirt floor. Though he was poor in worldly goods, he was rich in faith. The following story is one of the first miracle provisions God did for him. It also shows how God speaks specific directions to people even though they often do not make sense at the time.

> In 1964, I became engaged to my wife, Grace. At that time, I had absolutely nothing to give her as an engagement present. Our custom is to give your fiancée a special gift; I told her that I would give her a wristwatch. Then I began to calculate my net assets: a few bits of clothing (all well-used), a few study books and a Bible. In other words, I had nothing to sell to buy the watch. I prayed and asked JEHOVAH-JIREH to provide me with a watch for my future wife; then I began to calculate how God could answer my prayer...
>
> That Sunday, I preached with a heavy anointing from the Holy Spirit. Surely someone would be especially blessed and would hand me the watch God had provided. But no, nothing like that took place. The last person left and I had nothing. At the end of the night service, I also waited for my provision, but still nothing. What could I do? Well, I decided I would wait at the church until someone came.
>
> At that time, we had a twelve o'clock midnight curfew in Korea. No one could travel after midnight until morning, or they would be stopped by the police. I looked at the time in the church and saw that the hour was getting very close to midnight. I again prayed, "Father, You were JEHOVAH-JIREH to Abraham; I know You are the great provider. Won't You be my provider?" The answer

came to my heart, "Yes, I am your provider, too!" With that, peace came to my heart. I knew that God had the answer and had made provision. I was going to trust His Word, yet my mind was paying attention to the clock on the wall. Within a few minutes, the curfew would be in effect and no one would be able to come to the church and bring my watch.

Just before the midnight hour came, a knock came to our church door. My heart stopped as I wondered whether this was God's provision. I opened the door, and before me was an American gentleman in his pajamas. This man had been a soldier with the United States armed forces during the Korean War. He had been wounded, but had decided to stay in our country. He also attended our church. Although the wound had left him rather eccentric, he was a lovely Christian who really served God faithfully.

"What are you doing here at this time of night, brother," I asked him, seeing the look of perplexity on his face.

"Pastor Cho, I have a real problem," he answered me as he walked in the opened door.

Determined to get him out before he would have to spend the night at the church, I said, "Sir, if you think you have a problem, you don't know the problem I have. You had better go home right away before the beginning of the curfew and I will speak to you tomorrow!"

"No, pastor. Only you can solve my problem," he responded.

As the man walked towards my office, my only thoughts were on what I would tell Grace in the morning. I had promised my future wife that I would give her our engagement gift on Monday morning. What would I tell her? How could I expect her to marry me after I did not keep my promise? "Boy, what a mess I have gotten myself into," I thought as I sat down and tried to pay attention to what this American was going to share with me.

As he sat down, he looked at me and I could see the worried look on his face. I then figured that he had a real problem so I had better listen to him. However, my thoughts were on the look on Grace's face if I arrived in the morning without an engagement gift.

"Pastor Cho, I have a niece back home in America. Next week is her birthday. You know I love my family and so I tried to buy something for her that she would really enjoy."

"Please hurry up and get to the problem," I thought to myself; yet he continued to elaborate.

"Well, on Friday, I bought her a wristwatch. It is a real nice one and I got it for a good price at the PX."

"Yes," I said slowly, the story now becoming much more interesting.

"Tonight," he continued, "I was wrapping up the watch and the Holy Spirit began to speak to me."

"Please go on!" I said, my heart beginning to pound louder in my chest. Could this be my answer?" Could this be JEHOVAH-JIREH at work for me?

"This is my problem: The Holy Spirit spoke to me to give the watch to Pastor Cho, but I know that you are a bachelor and don't need a girl's watch. You could only use a man's watch. What can I do?"

After I explained my story, the man got so excited he began to dance around my office. "God really used me! God really used me!" he repeated over and over again. Both of us rejoiced as again God made provision in a way that I could have never imagined.[13]

CONCLUSION

If there is anything one can conclude from this chapter, it would be that God knows exactly where each one of us is. He knows the details of our lives right down to the coffee shops we visit, the airplanes we ride, and the tuition we need. He also wants to speak to us about those details. He speaks through His Word, the Bible, and through the Holy Spirit. Our job is to be in a position to hear and discern.

Don't let anyone intimidate you about hearing from God. —Henry Blackaby[14]

But the Helper, the Holy Spirit, whom the Father will send in My name, He will teach you all things... (John 14:26).

If you leave God's paths and go astray, you will hear a Voice behind you say, "No, this is the way; walk here" (Isaiah 30:21 TLB).

Chapter 7

A TRULY SUPERNATURAL BOOK

*The Bible—banned, burned, beloved. More widely read, more frequently attacked than any other book in history. Generations of intellectuals have attempted to discredit it; dictators of every age have outlawed it and executed those who read it. Yet soldiers carry it into battle believing it is more powerful than their weapons. Fragments of it smuggled into solitary prison cells have transformed ruthless killers into gentle saints. Pieced together scraps of Scripture have converted whole villages of pagan Indians. —*Charles Colson[1]

For centuries humanistic humankind has tried to stamp out the Bible's influence on civilization. Communist and Muslim countries have banned it. Intellectuals have ridiculed and attempted to discredit it. Throughout history, lovers of the Bible have been boiled in oil, burned at the stake, and beheaded. On August 1, 1556, in Derby, England, Joan Waste was burned at the stake for simply loving the Bible and the God it proclaimed. When Queen Mary took the throne, she created a new law making it illegal to own a Bible in English. But that didn't stop Joan and many others from smuggling Bibles into their homes and into their hearts. Because Joan couldn't hide her love for the Scriptures, she was discovered, dragged before the authorities, and thrown into prison. She was repeatedly interrogated and urged to give up the Bible reading and renounce her heresy. "I cannot forsake the truth," she finally said. "I beg you, please stop troubling me." From that point on she didn't open her mouth even as a death sentence was pronounced over her. Joan Waste was handed over to an executioner and marched to the stake like a convicted murderer. There, before a gathered group of onlookers, she dropped to her knees and prayed. When she stood back up, Joan looked out over the crowd. "Please pray for me," she urged. At that, the executioner secured her to the stake and lit the flames.[2]

Joan treasured the Bible all the way to her excruciating death because the truth within its pages had brought her great strength and unspeakable peace. During her five-year reign, Queen Mary executed over 280 Bible lovers by burning them at the stake. Ironically, Queen Mary died in 1558 at the young age of forty-two, but the Bible never died. It only continued to gain in popularity and power. That was over 450 years ago, and still today, in some areas of the world, men and women are imprisoned and tortured for refusing to give up their Bibles.

While writing this chapter, I came across the recent story of a converted Muslim in Bangladesh. Her English is rough, but listen to the words. I deleted the names and did not footnote for protection's sake.

> My father took the Bible that was in our room that we
> get from Pastor ____. He burned the Bible before us and
> said, "If you don't come back to Islam, I will burn you,
> your daughter _____ and son _____ like this Bible."
> We are in fear to be killed, and we cannot share these
> relatives for help because they are all Muslims and the
> police are also Muslims. _____, daughter of _____,
> said that now I read the Bible everyday, I get a new Bible
> from Pastor _____. We regularly pray. I pray that my
> father will one day feel the love of Christ. I forgive my

father as he beat me like dog, only for belief in Christ. I
don't fear to be burned like the Bible my father burned,
for my belief in Christ.

Even being beaten like a dog and threatened with burning didn't
keep this person from getting another Bible!

Consider this: To this day, despite ongoing attempts throughout
history to snuff it out, the Bible continues to be *the* number one
bestselling book of all time. In 1907, the *New York Times* reported
in an article titled, "The Book That Is the 'Best Seller,'" that the
Bible showed daily sales in excess of 40,000 copies![3] Year after year,
the Bible tops the bestseller lists with world sales of more than 100
million annually. Since book sales records have been kept, overall
sales of the Bible are somewhere in the neighborhood of 6 billion.
So many copies of the Bible are sold worldwide each year that it has
its own category.[4] The *British Times* said,

> Forget modern British novelists and TV tie-ins, the
> Bible is the best-selling book every year. If sales of the
> Bible were included in best-seller lists, it would be a rare
> week when anything else would achieve a look in. It
> is wonderful…that in this godless age…this one book
> should go on selling, every month.[5]

Even in countries where the Bible is outlawed and people can't
just walk into stores and purchase them, believers risk everything to
smuggle them across their borders and into their homes.

The question I want to ask is "Why?" Why is the Bible so popular? Why is it so polarizing? Why do some hate it so much that
they'd burn it along with its readers while others love it so much
they'd willingly die to protect it? Could it be that the Bible itself
is God's Word? Therefore, to some it is *"the aroma of death leading
to death, and* [to others, it's] *the aroma of life leading to life"* (2 Cor.
2:16). If God *is* real and the Bible *is* God's Word, then it makes perfect sense that the enemy would want to stamp it out? Yet because
it's God's Word, His power is behind it, and nothing can stop it.

That's why the Bible continues to be under attack, but still thrives and transforms the individuals who embrace it.

The Bible truly is a *supernatural* book. In fact, it is a self-contained miracle of its own. You could disregard all of the incredible stories that I've shared in this book and simply consider the overwhelming evidence built into the Bible alone and come to the firm conclusion that God is real and the Bible is His inspired Word to us. The Bible itself is one of God's greatest miracles. The rest of this chapter is dedicated to examination of some of the most convincing pieces of evidence.

While each individual piece is strong on its own, my goal is to lay a foundation that gradually builds in strength so that, at the end of the chapter, you will be able to pull all the pieces together, making an overwhelming case for inspiration. When one blows away all the smoke created by skeptics and considers the simple, straightforward evidence, it becomes very *sane* to conclude that the Bible is most definitely a *supernatural* book.

#1. THE BIBLE'S SUPERNATURAL UNITY

> Defend the Bible? I would just as soon defend a lion. Just turn the Bible loose. It will defend itself. —Charles H. Spurgeon

To begin with, we must consider the unbelievable unity of the Bible. It was penned by forty authors from diverse backgrounds living on three continents, stretched out over a period of sixteen centuries. A variety of kings, peasants, warriors, and priests wrote in a variety of languages—Hebrew, Greek, and Aramaic. Some were poets, some historians, some philosophers, and others biographers. Without any collaboration, what they produced was sixty-sixty books with 1,189 chapters that reveal in harmonious unity the unfolding of God's redemptive plan for humanity. How is this possible without supernatural guidance? Think about it in the following way. What are the odds that a group of writers who never met or talked to each other, who lived at different times and places in history, would produce one book that fits together with the precision of a five thousand piece jigsaw puzzle, producing one masterful, incredibly detailed picture? Dr. Erwin Lutzer described it this way:

> Imagine various pieces of a cathedral arriving from different countries and cities, converging on a central location. In fact, imagine that investigation proves that forty different sculptors made contributions over a period of many centuries. Yet the pieces fit together to form a single magnificent structure. Would this not be proof that behind the project was a single mind, one designer who used his workmen to sculpt a well-conceived plan? The Bible is that cathedral.[6]

It seems apparent that the Bible came from *One* mind that was manifest through forty different authors. And that, my friend, is quite supernatural!

#2. THE BIBLE'S SUPERNATURAL PRESERVATION AND TEXTUAL ACCURACY

> It's amazing that people try to argue that we cannot trust the Bible…But it would never occur to them to question the writings of Plato, Sophocles, Homer, or Caesar Augustus when we have fewer than ten copies of each book, and those copies were made at least 1,000 years after the author wrote the original. —Mark Driscoll[7]

Similar to the way the Bible defies the odds and continues, year after year, to dwarf other books in terms of sales, it also dwarfs other historical writings when it comes to preservation and textual accuracy. Evidence that the Bible has been preserved almost perfectly from the originals is greater than any other book in antiquity and, as you will see, not just by a little bit. There are two factors that come into play when establishing the reliability of ancient manuscripts—the actual number of copies we have of them and their age. Let's examine both to see how amazing this book is.

The Number of Biblical Manuscripts Compared to Other Historical Works

No one questions the historical reliability of such authors as Shakespeare, Plato, Caesar, or Homer. The following are the actual number of ancient manuscripts we have preserved of each, compared to the Bible.

- Plato's *Tetralogies*—7 copies

- Caesar's *Gallic Wars*—10 copies

- Aristotle's works—52 copies

- Homer's *Iliad*—643 copies

- *The New Testament*—5,700 handwritten Greek manuscripts and more than 9,000 in other languages (Syriac, Coptic, Latin, Arabic) in preservation.[8]

  In real terms, the New Testament is easily the best attested ancient writing in terms of the sheer number of documents, the time span between the events and the document, and the variety of documents available to sustain or contradict it. There is nothing in ancient manuscript evidence to match such textual availability and integrity. —Ravi K. Zacharias[9]

- *The Old Testament*—Over 10,000 ancient manuscripts preserved. (We'll see more on the Old Testament's reliability when we examine the Dead Sea Scrolls later in this section.)

How does the Bible compare with Shakespeare? According to Josh McDowell:

  Not only does the New Testament text have far superior evidence for reliability than the classics, it also is in better shape textually than the thirty-seven plays of William Shakespeare written in the seventeenth century after the invention of printing. In every one of Shakespeare's plays there are lacunae (gaps) in the printed text where we have no idea what originally was said. This forces textual scholars to make a conjectural emendation (a fancy term for 'good guess') to fill in the blank. With the abundance of manuscripts (handwritten copies) of the New Testament, nothing has been lost through the transmission of the text.[10]

The number of manuscripts we have in preservation is vital because the greater the number, the greater the accuracy. More copies means there are more to compare with and confirm what the originals say. Except for a few insignificant parts that have no relevance on the meaning, the thousands of Bible manuscripts we have match perfectly. The Bible is, hands down, the most accurate ancient text in existence.

The Age of the Biblical Manuscripts Compared to Other Historical Works

When using the term *age,* we are talking about the period of time that elapsed between when the original was written and when copies were made. In this regard, the biblical manuscripts are once again far superior to all other historical manuscripts.

- Plato's *Tetralogies* was written about 400 BC. The earliest copies we have date to AD 900, a time gap of 1,300 years.

- Caesar's *Gallic Wars* was written about 100-44 BC. The earliest copies we have date to AD 900, a time gap of 1,000 years.

- Aristotle's works were written about 350 BC. The earliest copies we have date from around AD 850, a time gap of roughly 1,150 years.

- Homer's *Iliad* was written about 800 BC. The earliest copies we have date to 400 BC, a time gap of 400 years.

- *The New Testament* was completed no later than AD 100, yet the earliest known complete manuscript dates to about 200 AD, a time gap of only about 100 years. However, we have a significant fragment of John's Gospel currently located in the John Rylands Library of Manchester, England, that has been dated to within fifty years of the date when the apostle John penned the original.[11]

The Old Testament and the Significance of the Dead Sea Scrolls

In 1947, the Dead Sea Scrolls were discovered in a group of secluded caves west of the Dead Sea in the Judean desert. Stored in sealed jars were over 900 scrolls (manuscripts) of the Old Testament written in both Hebrew and Aramaic. Somehow, miraculously perhaps, they had survived the depredation of time and were one thousand years older than the previous earliest manuscripts. It was as if those who put them there were guided by the hand of God to a place where they wouldn't be discovered for some two thousand years. Now here's the really exciting part! When the Dead Sea Scrolls were compared with the previous earliest manuscripts of the Old Testament, it was discovered that in one thousand years of copying, only one word differed. It's the word *light* in Isaiah 53:11. This tells us that the Old Testament stayed almost exactly the same for a thousand years. Only one word out of the entire manuscript had changed. That's quite impressive! The reason the Old Testament stayed so accurate is because devoted scribes, directed by God, followed a regiment that ensured precise transmission of the text. These scribes were called Masoretes. Below are the Masoretic guidelines for copying biblical text. God established these ten guidelines to ensure that His Word would be passed from one generation to the next.

1. The scribe could use only clean animal skins, both to write on and to bind manuscripts.

2. Each column of writing could have no less than forty-eight, and no more than sixty lines.

3. The ink must be black and of a special recipe.

4. The scribe must "verbalize" each word aloud while they were writing.

5. Nothing could be copied from memory; it had to be copied letter by letter.

6. The scribe must wipe the pen, and wash their entire bodies, before writing the word "Jehovah," every time they wrote it.

7. There must be a "review" within thirty days, and if as many as three pages required correction, the entire document had to be redone.

8. The letters, words, and paragraphs had to be counted, and the document became invalid if two letters touched each other. The middle paragraph, word, and letter must correspond to those of the original document.

9. The documents could be stored only in sacred places.

10. As no document containing God's Word could be destroyed, they were stored, or buried, in a *genizah*, a Hebrew term meaning "hiding place." These were usually kept in a synagogue or sometimes in a Jewish cemetery.[12]

By applying the same standards historians use for the evaluation of all historical documents, even the hardest of skeptics would have to admit that both the Old Testament and the New are light years above the rest when it comes to accuracy and reliability. I like the way ancient manuscript paleographer and Bible scholar Frederic Kenyon put it,

> The Christian can take the whole Bible in his hand and say without fear of hesitation that he holds in it the true Word of GOD, handed down without essential loss from generation to generation throughout the centuries...[13]

> This can be said of no other ancient book in the world.[14]

#3. ARCHEOLOGY CONTINUES TO CONFIRM THE BIBLE

> It may be stated categorically that no archaeological discovery has ever controverted a Biblical reference. Scores of archaeological findings have been made which confirm in clear outline or in exact detail historical statements in the Bible. —Dr. Nelson Glueck[15]

If the Bible *is* God's Word, then it should not only be spiritually true, but historically true as well—dealing with real places, real people, and actual events. After centuries and thousands of discoveries, not one single time has an archeological finding ever disproved the Bible. On the contrary, the more sophisticated the science of archeology becomes, the more the Bible is substantiated, time after time proving the critics wrong. There have been countless archeological discoveries that validate the Bible's highly specific records. It would take a whole volume to disclose them. Below are a few significant ones I chose to highlight because they confirm the Bible's exactness.

House of David Inscription

> *So Jonathan made a covenant with the **house of David**, saying, "Let the Lord require it at the hand of David's enemies"* (1 Samuel 20:16).

On July 21, 1993, a team of archeologists excavating at the ancient Israelite city of Dan stumbled upon a rare treasure. Unlike pottery and other "mute" artifacts commonly found at archeological digs, this was an inscription—a very important inscription. It was so significant that the discovery made the front page of the *New York Times*. What the team unearthed was a basalt stone that was part of a shattered monument, or *stele*. On the monument was an inscription memorializing the military victory of the king of Damascus over two ancient enemies: the King of Israel and the House of David.

This find was a historical bombshell because it was the first reference to King David from a non-biblical source. For years, critics of the Bible had contended that David was a mere legend, invented by Hebrew scribes. David and other heroes of the Bible, they argued, were about as historical as Hercules or Aladdin. But with this discovery, the skeptic's suffered a serious blow. There was now clear evidence of not only the existence of King David himself, but also his dynasty.[16]

The Stele of Mesha, King Omri

*...So all Israel made **Omri**, the commander of the army, king over Israel that day in the camp...**Omri** did evil in the eyes of the Lord, and did worse than all who were before him* (1 Kings 16:16,25).

On display in the Louvre museum, in Paris, is the Stele of Mesha. Mesha was the son of Kemoš-yatti, the king of Moab. The Moabites were arch archenemies of the Israelites. The Stele of Mesha is significant because it is a secular source that confirms the biblical account of King Omri listed in First Kings. The Bible says Omri, though he was an Israelite, did evil in God's sight. Like the Stele found at Dan, mentioning the House of David, the Mesha Stele commemorates Mesha's military victory over Omri. It also corroborates with the Bible that Omri was an oppressive king who oppressed the Moabites and that he did *"evil in the eyes of the Lord, and did worse than all who were before him."* Written in Tyrian text, the inscription on the basalt monument is lengthy and describes the events in detail. Below is a portion.

Translation of the Stele of Mesha

> I am Mesha, the son of Kemoš-yatti, the king of Moab, from Dibon. My father was king over Moab for thirty years, and I was king after my father.

> And in Karchoh I made this high place for Kemoš [...] because he has delivered me from all kings, and because he has made me look down on all my enemies.

> Omri was the king of Israel, and he oppressed Moab for many days, for Kemoš was angry with his land. And his son succeeded him, and he said—he too—"I will oppress Moab!" In my days he did so, but I looked down on him and on his house, and Israel has gone to ruin, yes, it has gone to ruin for ever![17]

Sargon the King of Assyria

> *In the year that Tartan came to Ashdod, when* **Sargon** *the king of Assyria sent him, and he fought against Ashdod and took it...* (Isaiah 20:1).

For years, critics asserted there was no Assyrian king named Sargon as recorded in Isaiah 20:1. However, yet again, archeology came to the rescue of the Bible, proving the skeptics wrong. In 1844, Sargon's palace was discovered in Khorsabad, Iraq. Chronicled on the walls of the palace is the capture of Ashdod, which is the actual event that Isaiah 20 mentions! On top of that, fragments of a *stela* memorializing the conquest were discovered at the city of Ashdod.

Today, the British Museum exhibits a collection of artifacts representing Sargon. One of the pieces is the "Sargon Vase," which bears an inscription with his name on it. The University of Chicago holds records and photographs of the numerous excavations at

Sargon's palace. The Vatican Museum has an inscribed brick from Sargon's palace in Khorsabad. The inscription commemorates the building of the city and of the palace:

> Sargon, king of the universe, built this city: Dûr-Shar-rûkin [The fortress of Sargon] is its name; inside it he had this unrivalled Palace built.[18]

The Belshazzar Cylinders

> **Belshazzar** *the king made a great feast for a thousand of his lords, and drank wine in the presence of the thousand... "And I have heard of you, that you can give interpretations and explain enigmas. Now if you can read the writing and make known to me its interpretation, you shall be clothed with purple and have a chain of gold around your neck,* ***and shall be the third ruler in the kingdom"*** (Daniel 5:1,16).

According to Daniel, Belshazzar was the king in Babylon who offered to promote him to third highest in command after he interpreted the handwriting that appeared mysteriously on the king's wall. Yet like Omri and Sargon, Belshazzar's name was not mentioned in non-biblical records so his existence was seriously doubted by critics. According to the non-biblical historic records, the last king of Babylon was Nabonidus.

But then archaeologists uncovered four small clay cylinders at Ur in Mesopotamia, inscribed with detailed accounts of the rebuilding of Ur's temple by King Nabonidus. The inscriptions also spoke of Nabonidus' eldest son and co-regent, Belshazzar! Additional tablets that have been found show numerous treaties and contracts that mention Belshazzar as well. This finding proved that Belshazzar did exist and served under his father as second in command. In which case, Belshazzar could offer to make Daniel the third highest ruler in the kingdom as this would have been the next highest available position. One more time, the Bible's record has been confirmed by archaeology.

The Philistines

Now there was no blacksmith to be found throughout all the land of Israel, for the Philistines said, "Lest the Hebrews make swords or spears." But all the Israelites would go down to the Philistines to sharpen each man's plowshare, his mattock, his ax, and his sickle (1 Samuel 13:19-20).

And a champion went out from the camp of the Philistines, named Goliath, from Gath, whose height was six cubits and a span. He had a bronze helmet on his head, and he was armed with a coat of mail, and the weight of the coat was five thousand shekels of bronze. And he had bronze armor on his legs and a bronze javelin between his shoulders. Now the **staff of his spear was like a weaver's beam,** *and his iron spearhead weighed six hundred shekels; and a shield-bearer went before him* (1 Samuel 17:4-7).

According to the Bible, the Philistines were more than just a major thorn in the side of the Israelites; they were their worst enemy. Militarily, the Philistines were more advanced, particularly because of their skill at metal-working that gave them the ability to craft superior weapons and armor. The problem for critics, like in the other cases, was that the Philistines did not appear in early ancient non-biblical sources. Again, they argued that the biblical stories of epic battles between the Israelites and the dreaded Philistines must have been fabricated by scribes to propagate the mythical empire of David.

Today, however, modern archaeology has confirmed that the Philistines did actually exist and were a superior military power for Israel to contend with. Archaeology has also established, through the uncovering of numerous bronze implements and artifacts, that the Philistines were indeed expert metallurgists with advanced skills compared to Israel, enabling them to control the metal-working trade during that era, just as the above passages allude to. This would be why it was necessary for the Hebrews to *"go down to the*

Philistines to sharpen each man's plowshare, his mattock, his ax, and his sickle" and the Philistines could thwart the Hebrew's ability to make spears and swords. In his book, *Is The Bible True?*, Jeffery Sheler notes the following:

> Trude Dothan, a Hebrew University archaeologist who has excavated many of the Philistine sites, says their superior knowledge of metal-working no doubt gave them a military advantage in their early battles with the Israelites. She notes that in the famous story of the duel between David and Goliath in 1 Samuel 17, the giant Philistine warrior is described as wearing a bronze helmet and bronze body-armor and carrying a spear with a shaft "like a weaver's beam" and with a head of iron. "The Bible compares Goliath's spear to a weaver's beam," Dothan says, "because this type of weapon was new to Canaan and had no Hebrew name."[19]

In addition to all of the above, a plethora of Egyptian inscriptions have been uncovered, pointing to Crete as the Philistines' original home. This lines up with biblical records as well. Jeremiah 47:4 says, *"Because of the day that comes to plunder all the Philistines...For the Lord shall plunder the Philistines, the remnant of the country of Caphtor."* Caphtor is a location that most scholars associate with Crete.

Each of the other cities prominently spoken of in the following Scripture regarding the Philistines have been positively identified and excavated. *"These are the golden tumors which the Philistines returned as a trespass offering to the Lord: one for Ashdod, one for Gaza, one for Ashkelon, one for Gath, one for Ekron"* (1 Sam. 6:17). Excavations in each of these sites yielded artifacts clearly associated with the Philistines. "In every instance," says Sheler, "the researchers found the archaeological data regarding the Philistines to be consistent with the biblical record."[20] William Dever, from the University of Arizona, says regarding the Philistines, "That all this 'fits' the many biblical allusions so well, shows that a post-Exilic editor cannot simply have invented these passages, that they are genuinely archaic."[21]

Pontius Pilate

Pontius Pilate being governor of Judaea... (Luke 3:1).

According to the New Testament, Pontius Pilate was the governor of Judaea and was the one who questioned Jesus and ultimately sentenced Him to death by crucifixion. For years, skeptics questioned the actual existence of a Roman governor by the name of Pontius Pilate. Then, in June 1961, archaeologists excavating an ancient Roman amphitheatre near Caesarea uncovered a curious limestone brick. On the face of the brick is an inscription that reads: "Pontius Pilate, Prefect of Judaea." Professor of New Testament Interpretation at Asbury Theological Seminary, Ben Witherington III, wrote in *Christianity Today* regarding the finding, "This provided inscriptional confirmation of the existence of Pilate and the role he played in Judea for over a decade (he is called a prefect in the inscription)."[22] The artifact is stored in the Israel Museum in Jerusalem, where its Inventory number is AE 1963 no. 104 and has been dated to the year AD 26–37.[23]

Before we move on from archeology, I would like to point out again that these are only a handful of thousands of archeological finds confirming the Bible. Some others worth mentioning are: The Hittites (see 2 Kings 7), the City of Nineveh, Herod's temple (see Luke 1:9), the Pool of Siloam (see John 9:7), Peter's house in Capernaum (see Matt. 8:14), Jacob's well (see John 4:5-6), the Artemis temple and altar (see Acts 19:27-28), the Sergius Paulus inscription (see Acts 13:6-7), the Derbe inscription (see Acts 14:20), the Ossuary of the high priest Caiaphas (see Matt. 26:3), the Pergamon Altar—Satan's Throne (see Rev. 2:12-13), and James brother of Jesus' Ossuary.

By the time this book comes off the press, it is likely that even more amazing discoveries will have been uncovered.

Every year more and more Bible skeptics are becoming discredited as solid archeological evidence is turning their speculations of doubt into fabrications born from a rebellious mind. If we don't Praise and Glorify God, "Even the Rocks will Cry out." (Luke 19:37-40)...And through archaeology they are! —Hilton Harrell Jr.[24]

#4. SCIENCE CONTINUES TO CONFIRM AND CATCH UP WITH THE BIBLE

No sciences are better attested to than the science of the Bible. —Sir Isaac Newton[25]

As with archeology, the more advanced the other sciences become, the more the Bible is confirmed. And, just as with archeology, science has never once disproved the Bible. While the Bible is not a science book, it does make statements that are scientifically accurate. I'm not saying that science is "proving" the Bible, but that the Bible has been consistent with scientific discoveries over the years, as it has been with archeology. Because the Bible is not trying to "prove" anything, it speaks of scientific matters in a simple, natural manner. Still, the fact of the matter is that science is, in many cases, finally catching up with the Bible. On numerous occasions, science assumed the Bible was wrong, only to later, as science progressed, discover that the Bible was correct after all. The following are a few examples of how the Scriptures declared something scientifically profound long before the scientific method revealed it as fact. You can decide what you want to believe.

People Are Made From the Dust of the Ground

And the Lord God formed man of the dust of the ground, and breathed into his nostrils the breath of life; and man became a living being (Genesis 2:7).

For years, the scientific community dismissed and often ridiculed the apparent childlike simplicity of the Bible's claim that God created humankind from *"the dust of the ground."* Well, they aren't dismissing it anymore. After over a century of growth and development in the field of human anatomy, scientists have discovered that the elements found within the human body are the same as those found in dirt and clay. In 1982, after an in-depth study, researchers at NASA's Ames Research Center confirmed that every single element found in the human body is also present in dirt. "We are just beginning to learn," the scientists acknowledged. "The biblical scenario for the creation of life turns out to be not far off the mark."[26] According to Bill Size, the associate professor and director of the Geosciences Program, interim director of the Human and Natural Ecology Program, and chairman of the Senate committee on the environment,

> The earth's crust contains most of the mineral nutrients our body needs, and the chemical composition of a rock, such as granite, is strikingly similar to the composition of the human body.[27]

An article in the *Scientific American* puts it:

> Welcome or not, dying is a natural part of the circle of life. Death initiates a complex process by which the human body gradually reverts *back* to dust, *as it were.*[28]

Bible Declares Empty Hole in Space

He spreads out the northern skies over empty space… (Job 26:7 NIV).

A short time ago, astronomers discovered that the space due north of the Earth's axis in the vicinity of the North Star and the constellation Bootes is relatively empty of stars compared to other areas of space. For centuries, this "emptiness" in space could not be detected with the naked eye. Only after the development of high powered telescopes was it discovered. Mitchell Waldrop wrote about the phenomenon in *Science Magazine*.

The recently announced "hole in space," a 300-million light-year gap in the distribution of galaxies, has taken cosmologists by surprise...[an area] in the Northern Hemisphere, lying in the general direction of the constellation Bootes, showed striking gaps...[29]

After being discovered in 1981 by Robert Kirshner of the Harvard-Smithsonian Center for Astrophysics, this expanse of nothingness is now known as the *Bootes Void*. God, of course, knew about it all along and stated such in the Book of Job.

The Wind Has Weight

For He looks to the ends of the earth, and sees under the whole heavens, to establish a weight for the wind, and apportion the waters by measure. When He made a law for the rain, and a path for the thunderbolt... (Job 28:24-26).

Once upon a time, air was considered weightless, but then in 1643 Italian scientist Evangelista Torricelli discovered a little thing called barometric pressure. What the good scientist figured out was that if air could support a column of water twenty-six feet high, then it should support a column of mercury about two feet high because mercury is thirteen times as heavy as water. Torricelli devised a mercury barometer and proved that air has pressure, or weight. Yet the Bible declared the wind had weight about four thousand years ago. The Bible also showed that this weight of the wind, or barometric pressure, affects the weather patterns, something meteorologists use every day.

Matthew Maury, the father of oceanography said it this way:

Though the fact that the air has weight is here so distantly announced [in Job], philosophers never recognized the fact until within comparatively a recent period, and then it was proclaimed by them as a great discovery. Nevertheless, the fact was set forth as distinctly in the book of nature as it is in the book of revelation; for the infant, in availing itself of atmospherical pressure to draw milk from its mother's breast, unconsciously proclaimed it.[30]

Gulf Stream and Paths Under the Ocean

The birds of the air, and the fish of the sea, that pass through the paths of the seas (Psalm 8:8).

The above Scripture declares that there are paths in the seas. The word *paths* here actually indicates currents or rivers that flow through the oceans. This may seem old news to us today; however, it wasn't until the late 1700s that Benjamin Franklin began to study the prospect of ocean currents, which included in-depth interviews with ocean ship captains. In 1786, he published his findings that revealed massive currents or paths running under the ocean's surface. One such path was the Gulf Stream, which moves about five-thousand more times the amount of water than the Mississippi River. Later, scientists discovered that the Gulf Stream is only part of a huge system of currents that flow through all of the oceans and have a profound effect upon the Earth's climate.

As I stated in the previous section, Matthew Maury is known by many as the father of oceanography. He was elected to the Hall of Fame for Great Americans, and a monument was erected in his honor in Richmond, Virginia. The inscription on it reads: "Matthew Fontaine Maury, Pathfinder of the Seas, the genius who first snatched from the oceans and atmosphere the secret of their laws." Maury was a naval oceanographer and in 1842 was appointed superintendent of the US Naval Observatory in Washington and also of the US Depot of Charts and Instruments. After reading Psalm 8, particularly the words, *"That pass through the paths of the seas,"* Maury determined that if God's Word said there were "paths" in the seas, then there must be paths. So he set out to find them. His search took over a decade, and what he discovered changed the science of marine navigation forever. From his studies and experiments, he compiled charts revealing the "paths" of the seas. These charts drastically increased the speed of ocean vessels, cutting their sailing time. In 1847, he published the book *Wind and Current Charts*. Then in 1856, Maury published his first textbook on modern oceanography, *The Physical Geography of the Sea and Its Meteorology*. God was right, and Maury confirmed it!

The Pleiades and Orion Star Clusters Described Before Telescopes

Can you bind the beautiful Pleiades? Can you loose the cords of Orion? (Job 38:31 NIV)

At the time of Job, there were no high-powered telescopes like we have today. So the stars and constellations could only be observed by the naked eye. Pleiades and Orion are clusters of stars that God gave Job details about before it was known scientifically. The writings of Job say that the Pleiades star cluster is "bound together." Using a high-powered telescope, one can see today that the stars are bound by gravity and are not breaking away. It is more common to see star clusters expanding like in Orion. God asks Job if he can loose the cords or bands of Orion. Today one can see the Orion star system is steadily expanding outward, as was written in Scripture long before it could be seen. God spoke to Job of scientific facts in the heavens before it could be known or explained by humans.

Perfect Ship Dimensions

And this is how you shall make it: The length of the ark [shall be] three hundred cubits, its width fifty cubits, and its height thirty cubits (Genesis 6:15).

When the Bible gives specific dimensions to build something, we best take note. Noah's Ark is no exception. Its dimensions are perfect for a stable cargo ship. I live a few miles from the Mississippi River and often go to the levee to walk. Each time I go, I see massive barges loaded to the hilt with heavy, expensive materials moving up and down the river. The reason they can be loaded down with so much weight is because they are almost impossible to sink. Ship builders today are well aware that the ultimate dimension for ship stability is a length six times that of the width. That's the general dimension of a barge and the same dimensions God gave Noah back in Genesis.

In 1993, Dr. Seon Hong headed up a scientific study on the construction of Noah's Ark. This was no amateurish study. Dr. Hong earned a BS degree in naval architecture from Seoul National University and a PhD in applied mechanics from the University of Michigan, Ann Arbor. What his study found was nothing short of fascinating. He and his research team concluded that the proportions of Noah's Ark were flawlessly balanced in the three main needs of modern cargo vessels—stability (resistance to capsizing), comfort "seakeeping," and strength. Various hydrodynamic tests confirmed that it was virtually impossible to capsize, even with waves of one hundred feet. Yet if the dimensions were altered even slightly, the vessel became either unstable, prone to rupture, or hazardously uncomfortable. By the way, in 2005 Dr. Hong was appointed Director General of the Maritime and Ocean Engineering Research Institute in Korea.[31]

The Scripps Institute of Oceanography in La Jolla, California, conducted a buoyancy and stability study on the dimensions of Noah's Ark. What they concluded, as with Dr. Hong's study, was that the Ark proved practically impossible to capsize. A scale model of the Ark was built and tested in a tank with a wave-generating machine. The affect of hyper-wave action on the scale model was proportionately larger than any storm could produce.[32] It turns out that this design is a perfect design to prevent capsizing in rough seas. Once again, it appears that science lines up with the Bible. It seems inconceivable that ancient writers would be able to conceive of a boat of such perfection and magnitude without divine inspiration.

The Universe Had a Beginning

In the beginning God created the heavens and the earth (Genesis 1:1).

If you haven't been living under a rock for the past hundred years, then you know science has confirmed the biblical view that the universe had a beginning. Einstein, Relativity, Boom! The Big Bang! Since Einstein, we've continued to learn that the universe is expanding out from a single point or beginning in time. The whole phenomenon of time is because the universe is moving. That would make God, if He did create the universe, outside of time, just like the Bible says. Science also confirms that as we approach the speed of light, time slows down. Hummm. So if, in theory, we could live at the speed of light, there would be no time. If God exists in light and is the source of light itself, and if we could exist in His light, then time would cease for us. Hummm. That sounds a lot like eternity—eternal life. I know. I'm stretching it a bit. But I can't help it. I get excited. The bottom line is, today scientists accept as fact that the universe burst into existence at a particular point in time and is rapidly expanding at a staggering speed. Dr. P. Dirac, a Nobel Prize-winner from Cambridge University, wrote: "It seems certain that there was a definite time of creation."[33] Here in Genesis 1:1, the Bible avows in simple, straightforward terms an obvious scientific reality, as if God didn't have a single thing to prove.

The Ocean Floor Contains Springs

Hast thou entered into the springs of the sea? or hast thou walked in the search of the depth? (Job 38:16 KJV)

Springs in the sea? The Hebrew word for *springs* in this verse is *nebek,* which refers to the places where water erupts forth from the Earth. This is another one that must've made Job scratch his head. If there were springs in the sea, Job certainly couldn't have known it. I mean, the ocean is deep, very deep, miles and miles deep. On top of that, the ocean floor is in complete darkness and under immense pressure. It would have been totally impossible for Job to enter the depths of the sea. There were no submarines or deep sea diving apparatuses or sonar or lights to do deep sea exploration. Yet there it is in black and white. "Hey Job man, have you been on the floor of the oceans? Did you know I put springs down there where you or the rest of humankind won't possibly be able to see or even explore until around the twentieth century?"

Until recently, it was thought that oceans were fed only by rivers and rain. In the 1930s, the deep sea explorations of William Beebe provided the first real close-up looks of the ocean floor, but no ocean springs were observed. By the 1940s, undersea topography was beginning to develop with the aid of the echo sounder. Thousands of underwater volcanoes were discovered, but still no "springs," though speculation about them grew. Over the next thirty-five years, underwater exploration evolved along with technology. By the mid-1970s, oceanographers were working with deep diving research submarines constructed to withstand six thousand pounds-per-square-inch pressure. Finally, with the help of such equipment, deep sea springs were finally discovered! An article in the November 1979 issue of *National Geographic* bore the caption: "Scientists explore rifts in the seafloor where hot springs spew minerals and startling life exists in a strange world without sun."[34] A January 12, 1980 article in *Science News* proclaimed: "Sea floor oases of mineral-rich springs and amazing creatures fulfill oceanographers' dreams."[35] The discovery of these deep ocean springs is said to be the "most significant oceanographic find since the discovery of the Mid-Atlantic Ridge."[36] God knew about them all along.

The Earth Free-Floats in Space, Affected Only by Gravity

He hangs the earth on nothing (Job 26:7).

This is a pretty amazing statement of fact. The Earth is suspended in space. Nothing tangible holds it up. At that time, just like Job couldn't search the depths of the sea, he had no idea about the gravitational attraction between the Earth and the sun. The majority of humanity believed the Earth was flat until the days of Columbus. Remember, the skeptics were sure Columbus' ships were going to sail right off the edge of the Earth. At the time of Job, some religious writings even declared that the earth sat on the back of an elephant or turtle or was held up by Atlas. But the Bible alone states what we now know to be true from the beginning. Like God created the universe, *"He hangs the earth on nothing."*

Numbered Hairs

> *And even the very hairs of your head are all numbered* (Matthew 10:30 NIV).

How could this be? When Jesus made that statement, He meant exactly what He said. Our hairs are numbered. It simply took science centuries to confirm what God already knew. The answer lies in our DNA. Each strand of DNA located within each individual cell contains a highly detailed genetic code that determines everything from the color of our eyes to the length of our toes to our talents and tendencies. Our DNA is like a complex program, which, if we were to load it onto a computer, would produce an elaborate design along with a detailed plan for our assembly! Each single strand of DNA contains so much information that scientists who study genetics realize that the information encoded in an individual's DNA contains data equivalent to a thousand encyclopedias. The sheer volume of information is staggering and points clearly to a God who is infinitely more knowledgeable than any Nobel Prize-winning scientist. Scientists can get an enormous amount of data from just a single strand of hair. Since it holds all your genetic information in the form of DNA, one strand of hair can identify you easily!

Science attests to the supernatural Bible.

#5. AMAZING PINPOINT PROPHECIES THAT ONLY GOD COULD HAVE KNOWN

> Even the most skeptical person can put the Bible to the test by noting the literal, precise fulfillment of past prophecies. —Mark Hitchcock, ThM, PhD[37]

As you can see, our case for the Bible is building. Now we are going to dive into a most miraculous element of Scripture—the fulfillment of highly specific, detailed prophecies concerning cities, nations, and kings in ancient history—prophecies that no person could have guessed. Of course, entire books have been written on biblical prophecy. My goal in this section is to highlight some of the most impressive ones that leave absolutely no other explanation but the supernatural hand of God.

Tyre will be thrown into the sea and become a place for the spreading of nets.

> *Therefore thus says the Lord God, "Behold, I am against you, O Tyre, and will cause many nations to come up against you, as the sea causes its waves to come up. And they shall destroy the walls of Tyre and break down her towers; I will also scrape her dust from her, and make her like the top of a rock. It shall be a place for spreading nets in the midst of the sea, for I have spoken," says the Lord God…"They will lay your stones, your timber, and your soil in the midst of the water….and you shall never be rebuilt, for I the Lord have spoken"* (Ezekiel 26:3-5,12,14).

Tyre was a great Phoenician city of international commerce on the Mediterranean Sea. There was the mainland city on the coast and an island city that was a military stronghold about a half mile off the coast. A massive wall 150 feet high and 25 feet wide circled the city. Full of sin and idols, Tyre was wealthy, proud, and self-secure. It was at its peak. But in about 587 BC, against logic, Ezekiel prophesied (#1) that the great city would be destroyed, (#2) its stones and timber would be thrown into the sea, (#3) it would be scraped so clean that it would be become a place for fishermen to spread out their nets to dry, and (#4) it would never be rebuilt—four very specific prophetic elements. Each one must be fulfilled precisely for it to be considered a supernatural act of God.

In 585 BC, just two years after Ezekiel's prophecy, Nebuchadnezzar of Babylon laid siege to Tyre in an assault that lasted thirteen years. Tyre put up a good fight, but eventually the city succumbed and many were killed. Thousands, however, fled to the island city in the sea. The inland city had been reduced to rubble. Tons of stone, bricks, and timbers remained from the destruction, but the island stronghold had survived. It appeared that only a minor part of Ezekiel's prophecy had been fulfilled. Only half of Tyre had been destroyed. Its timber and stone had not been cast into the sea, and island Tyre was still a functioning city. Certainly, it had not been scraped clean like the top of a rock for fishermen to cast their nets.

For the next 250 years, the city of Tyre thrived. Ezekiel had long since died, and it appeared his prophecy had as well. But God wasn't dead—and He wasn't finished. In 332 BC, Alexander the Great, with his thirst for conquest, came along. Alexander couldn't have known that he was merely a tool in God's hands. The great military leader led his army to the Mediterranean Sea and eventually to the island city of Tyre. There he commanded the city to surrender. When they laughed at this, thinking their stronghold was impregnable, Alexander did something that no one could have seen coming. He had his army gather up the remains from the inland city to use as materials to build a massive causeway across the half mile stretch of water to the island. The army collected millions of tons of rubble, timbers, and stones, literally casting them into the sea. What remained of Tyre was scraped clean like the top of a rock to make the highway. For centuries the ancient city lay in waste and was never rebuilt. Today there is a modern city of Tyre, but it is a modest fishing village located some distance from the ancient location. Archaeological excavations have confirmed that no city has been rebuilt over the ruins of Tyre, which is a fulfillment of this prophecy. Renowned archaeologist Hans-Wolf Rackl noted, "Today hardly a single stone of the old Tyre is intact. Tyre has become a place 'to dry fish nets.'"[38]

Today if you visit the location of the one-time city of Tyre, you will see that Hans-Wolf Rackl was correct. It is a place where local fishermen spread out their nets for drying. All four specific points to

Ezekiel's prophecy came to pass, exactly, over a period of centuries in a way that no person could have imagined. This one prophecy alone proves beyond any doubt that God is alive! And it all happened because God said, *"I the Lord have spoken."*

Jerusalem will be burned, and King Cyrus is called by name 100 years before his birth, 160 years before his reign!

In 626 BC, Jeremiah prophesied that Israel would be taken captive by King Nebuchadnezzar of Babylon and that Jerusalem and the temple would be destroyed by fire. At the time of Jeremiah's warning, Jerusalem and the temple were standing strong and secure.

Jeremiah's amazingly specific prophecy, 626 BC:

> *"Behold, I am the Lord, the God of all flesh. Is there anything too hard for Me?" Therefore thus says the Lord: "Behold, I will give this city* [Jerusalem] *into the hand of the Chaldeans* [Babylonians], ***into the hand of Nebuchadnezzar king of Babylon,*** *and he shall take it. And the Chaldeans who fight against this city* **shall come and set fire to this city and burn it,** *with the houses on whose roofs they have offered incense to Baal and poured out drink offerings to other gods, to provoke Me to anger; because the children of Israel and the children of Judah have done only evil before Me for from their youth…"* (Jeremiah 32:27-30).

The dramatic fulfillment happened in 587 BC. Roughly forty years later, just as Jeremiah had predicted, Nebuchadnezzar and his army strode into Jerusalem, burned it to the ground, and enslaved its inhabitants. On many fronts, archeology has confirmed the rule of Nebuchadnezzar and the destruction of Jerusalem.

Jeremiah predicted in striking detail what would happen to Jerusalem forty years in advance. Now, here's where it gets really cool. About one hundred years before Jeremiah made his prediction, Isaiah prophesied that a man named Cyrus would come along and that

God would use him to free Israel from their captivity to Babylon and release them back to Jerusalem to rebuild the city and temple. Do you see the incredible irony in all of this? God prophesied His plan of redemption to Israel well before Jeremiah prophesied the actual destruction of the city and captivity. According to Isaiah's prophecy, a man named Cyrus would be raised up and become king of the Persian Empire. He would then be guided by the hand of God to defeat the Babylonians, release the children of Israel from their captivity, and send them back to Jerusalem to rebuild the temple. All this was prophesied over 100 years before Cyrus was even born and 160 years before he became King! On top of that, at the time of Isaiah's prophecy, the city of Jerusalem and temple were standing strong so it wouldn't even make sense to talk about rebuilding it. But years later, in 586 BC, just as Jeremiah had predicted, Jerusalem was overtaken by Babylonian King Nebuchadnezzar. About forty-seven years later, however, in 539 BC, the Persians took over. Shortly thereafter, again just as Isaiah predicted, the Persian King Cyrus released Israel and gave the decree to rebuild the temple in Jerusalem. This is another example of history fulfilling future events prophesied in the Scripture!

The prophecy by Isaiah, 700 BC:

> It is I who says of **Cyrus**, He is my shepherd! And he will perform all My desire. And he declares of Jerusalem, "She will be built," and of the temple, "Your foundation will be laid." Thus says the Lord to **Cyrus** His anointed, whom I have taken by the right hand, to **subdue nations before him and to loose the loins of kings**; to open doors before him so that gates will not be shut (Isaiah 44:28–45:1 NASB).

The dramatic fulfillment of the prophecy over 160 years later in 539 BC:

> Now in the first year of Cyrus king of Persia—in order to fulfill the word of the Lord by the mouth of Jeremiah—the Lord stirred up the spirit of Cyrus king of Persia, so that he sent a proclamation throughout his kingdom, and also put

it in writing, saying, "Thus says Cyrus king of Persia, 'The Lord, the God of heaven, has given me all the kingdoms of the earth, and He has appointed me to build Him a house in Jerusalem, which is in Judah. Whoever is among you of all His people, may the Lord his God be with him, and let him go up'" (2 Chronicles 36:22-23 NASB).

The Cyrus Cylinder Discovery

Ancient clay cylinders dating to the sixth century BC were discovered in the ruins of Babylon in modern-day Iraq. The above conquest by King Cyrus and release of the Israelites and other nations held in captivity was recorded on this non-biblical record now known as the Cyrus Cylinder. Concerning the inscription on the cylinder, respected biblical scholar and archeologist Merrill Unger said, "This royal edict shows that Cyrus intervened and reversed the inhumane policy of displacing whole populations as practiced by the Assyrian and Babylonian conquerors."[39]

How could Jeremiah possibly know forty years in advance that Jerusalem would be burned and taken over by Babylon except by the Spirit of God? And how could Isaiah possibly know 160 years ahead of time that a man named Cyrus would be born, become king, and be used of God to set Israel free except by the Sprit of God?

Skeptics, of course, who attack the Bible with an anti-supernatural bias, try to assert that the fulfilled prophecies, like those of Jeremiah and Isaiah, were written after the fact. However, with what we know from the confirmations of archeology, the practices of prophets, and the strict Masoretic rules of the scribes, it's highly unlikely that such modifications would have been made. Old Testament scholar Alfred Martin tells it this way:

> This is actually the crux of the problem as far as the attitude of critics toward the Book of Isaiah is concerned…
> Here is Isaiah in the eighth century B.C. announcing Cyrus as the restorer of the people to Jerusalem, Cyrus who lived in the sixth century B.C. The whole point

of the passage is that God, the omniscient God, is the One who announces events beforehand. That is the proof of His deity. The destructive critics who say this passage must have been written in the sixth century by some otherwise unknown prophet in Babylon ("Deutero-Isaiah") are making the same stupid mistake that the idolaters of Isaiah's day were making. They are like the Sadducees of anther time, to whom the Lord Jesus Christ said, "Ye do err, not knowing the scriptures, nor the power of God" (Matthew 22:39 KJV).[40]

#6. AMAZING MESSIANIC PROPHECIES AND FULFILLMENTS

It would take a Jesus to forge a Jesus, and if it is true that what we have in the Bible is a giant forgery, then let us worship the individual who was so brilliant as to think up a picture of a person like Jesus of Nazareth and the story of the Word of God. —French skeptic Ernest Renan[41]

The accuracy of the Old Testament prophecies regarding Tyre and Cyrus are impressive, but even more so are those prophecies regarding the coming Messiah, Jesus Christ. When examining the Old Testament from Genesis to Malachi, it becomes indisputable that the book's overall message is Christ-centered. Remember that supernatural unity of forty-four authors writing over sixteen centuries producing one masterful, incredibly detailed picture? That picture is God's plan of redemption through the Messiah, Jesus Christ.

When the early Church was being birthed, following the crucifixion and resurrection of Jesus, the apostles preached their messages from the Old Testament. There was no New Testament. They took the Old Testament and showed the Jews and Gentiles Jesus within its pages. Acts chapter 8 demonstrates this perfectly. In this passage, an Ethiopian eunuch was in his chariot reading the Book of Isaiah and was having difficulty understanding it. Philip, being led by the Spirit, began to explain it to him, showing him Jesus in the text. Listen to the Scripture.

> So [Philip] *arose and went. And behold, a man of Ethiopia, a eunuch of great authority under Candace the queen of the Ethiopians, who had charge of all her treasury, and had come to Jerusalem to worship, was returning. And sitting in his chariot, he was reading Isaiah the prophet. Then the Spirit said to Philip, "Go near and overtake this chariot." So Philip ran to him, and heard him reading the prophet Isaiah, and said, "Do you understand what you are reading?" And he said, "How can I, unless someone guides me?" And he asked Philip to come up and sit with him. The place in the Scripture which he read was this:*

> *"He was led as a sheep to the slaughter; and as a lamb before its shearer is silent, so He opened not His mouth. In His humiliation His justice was taken away, and who will declare His generation? For His life is taken from the earth."*

> *So the eunuch answered Philip and said, "I ask you, of whom does the prophet say this, of himself or of some other man?" Then Philip opened his mouth, and beginning at this Scripture, preached Jesus to him* (Acts 8:27-35).

Jesus fulfilled over one hundred Old Testament prophecies. I picked only the most incredible ones to share, which date from about 1000 BC forward.

1. BORN IN BETHLEHEM EPHRATHAH (EPHRATHAH IS THE ANCIENT NAME FOR JUDAH)

Prophecy, 700 BC:

> *But you, Bethlehem Ephrathah, though you are little among the thousands of Judah, yet out of you shall come forth to Me*

the One to be Ruler in Israel, whose goings forth are from of old, from everlasting (Micah 5:2).

Fulfillment:

Now after Jesus was born in Bethlehem of Judea in the days of Herod the king, behold, wise men from the East came to Jerusalem, saying, "Where is He who has been born King of the Jews? For we have seen His star in the East and have come to worship Him." When Herod the king heard this, he was troubled, and all Jerusalem with him. And when he had gathered all the chief priests and scribes of the people together, he inquired of them where the Christ was to be born. So they said to him, "In Bethlehem of Judea, for thus it is written by the prophet: 'But you, Bethlehem, in the land of Judah, are not the least among the rulers of Judah; for out of you shall come a Ruler who will shepherd My people Israel'" (Matthew 2:1-6).

Over the years, there have been a number of Bethlehems in Israel. At the time of Jesus' birth, Bethlehem Ephrathah, referred to in Matthew as "Bethlehem in Judea," was a village about five miles south of Jerusalem, and there also was a town named Bethlehem about seven miles northwest of Nazareth.[42]

2. BETRAYED FOR THIRTY PIECES OF SILVER

Prophecy, 500 BC:

Then I said to them, "If it is agreeable to you, give me my wages; and if not, refrain." So they weighed out for my wages thirty pieces of silver (Zechariah 11:12).

Fulfillment:

Then one of the twelve, called Judas Iscariot, went to the chief priests and said, "What are you willing to give me if

I deliver Him to you?" And they counted out to him thirty pieces of silver (Matthew 26:14-15).

3. BETRAYAL MONEY CAST TO THE FLOOR OF THE TEMPLE

Prophecy:

And the Lord said to me, "Throw it to the potter"—that princely price they set on me. So I took the thirty pieces of silver and threw them into the house of the Lord for the potter (Zechariah 11:13).

Fulfillment:

Then he threw down the pieces of silver in the temple and departed... (Matthew 27:5).

4. BETRAYAL MONEY USED TO BUY THE POTTER'S FIELD

Prophecy:

*And the Lord said to me, "Throw it to the potter"—that princely price they set on me. So I took the thirty pieces of silver and threw them into the house of the Lord **for the potter*** (Zechariah 11:13).

Fulfillment:

And they consulted together and bought with them the potter's field, to bury strangers in (Matthew 27:7).

5. BEATEN WITH A ROD

Prophecy, 700 BC:

...They will strike the judge of Israel with a rod on the cheek (Micah 5:1).

Fulfillment:

Then they struck Him on the head with a reed and spat on Him; and bowing the knee, they worshiped Him (Mark 15:19).

6. GIVEN VINEGAR AND GALL TO DRINK

Prophecy, 1000 BC:

They also gave me gall for my food, and for my thirst they gave me vinegar to drink (Psalm 69:21).

Fulfillment:

They gave Him sour wine [vinegar] *mingled with gall to drink. But when He had tasted it, He would not drink* (Matthew 27:34).

Immediately one of them ran and took a sponge, filled it with sour wine and put it on a reed, and offered it to Him to drink (Matthew 27:48).

7. NO BONES BROKEN

Prophecy, 1000 BC:

He guards all his bones; not one of them is broken (Psalm 34:20).

Fulfillment:

But when they came to Jesus and saw that He was already dead, they did not break His legs (John 19:33).

It is important to realize that crucifixion victims' legs *normally* were broken. Yet *a thousand years* before the crucifixion of Jesus, King David foretold that *the Messiah* would have no broken bones, which is very significant for the way Jesus was killed.

8. BURIED IN A RICH MAN'S TOMB

Prophecy, 700 BC:

> *And they made His grave with the wicked—but with the rich at His death* (Isaiah 53:9).

Fulfillment:

> *Now when evening had come, there came a rich man from Arimathea, named Joseph, who himself had also become a disciple of Jesus…When Joseph had taken the body, he wrapped it in a clean linen cloth, and laid it in his new tomb which he had hewn out of the rock; and he rolled a large stone against the door of the tomb, and departed* (Matthew 27:57,59-60).

9. HANDS AND FEET NAILED

Prophecy, 1000 BC:

> *…The congregation of the wicked has enclosed Me. They pierced My hands and My feet* (Psalm 22:16).

Fulfillment:

> *And when they had come to the place called Calvary, there they crucified Him* (Luke 23:33).

10. ENTERED JERUSALEM ON A DONKEY

Prophecy:

> *Rejoice greatly, O daughter of Zion! Shout, O daughter of Jerusalem! Behold, your King is coming to you; He is just and having salvation, lowly and riding on a donkey, a colt, the foal of a donkey* (Zechariah 9:9).

Fulfillment:

> *Then they brought him to Jesus. And they threw their own clothes on the colt, and they set Jesus on him* (Luke 19:35).

11. BETRAYED BY A FRIEND

Prophecy:

> *Even my familiar friend in whom I trusted, who ate my bread, has lifted up his heel against me* (Psalm 41:9).

Fulfillment:

> *And supper being ended, the devil having already put it into the heart of Judas Iscariot, Simon's son, to betray Him* (John 13:2).

12. WOUNDED AND BRUISED

Prophecy:

> *But He was wounded for our transgressions, He was bruised for our iniquities* (Isaiah 53:5).

Fulfillment:

> *Then he released Barabbas to them; and when he had scourged Jesus, he delivered Him to be crucified* (Matthew 27:26).

13. SILENT BEFORE HIS ACCUSERS

Prophecy:

> *He was oppressed and He was afflicted, yet He opened not His mouth; He was led as a lamb to the slaughter, and as a*

sheep before its shearers is silent, so He opened not His mouth (Isaiah 53:7).

Fulfillment:

And while He was being accused by the chief priests and elders, He answered nothing (Matthew 27:12).

14. MOCKED, RIDICULED, AND REJECTED

Prophecy:

He is despised and rejected by men, a Man of sorrows and acquainted with grief. And we hid, as it were, our faces from Him; He was despised, and we did not esteem Him (Isaiah 53:3).

Fulfillment:

Then the soldiers of the governor took Jesus into the Praetorium and gathered the whole garrison around Him. And they stripped Him and put a scarlet robe on Him. When they had twisted a crown of thorns, they put it on His head, and a reed in His right hand. And they bowed the knee before Him and mocked Him, saying, "Hail, King of the Jews!" Then they spat on Him, and took the reed and struck Him on the head. And when they had mocked Him, they took the robe off Him, put His own clothes on Him, and led Him away to be crucified (Matthew 27:27-31).

15. STARED AT

Prophecy:

*I can count all My bones. They look and **stare at Me*** (Psalm 22:17).

Fulfillment:

And the people stood looking on. But even the rulers with them sneered, saying, "He saved others; let Him save Himself if He is the Christ, the chosen of God" (Luke 23:35).

16. LOTS CAST FOR HIS GARMENTS

Prophecy:

They divide My garments among them, and for My clothing they cast lots (Psalm 22:18).

Fulfillment:

Then the soldiers, when they had crucified Jesus, took His garments and made four parts, to each soldier a part, and also the tunic. Now the tunic was without seam, woven from the top in one piece. They said…,"Let us not tear it, but cast lots for it, whose it shall be" (John 19:23-24).

17. PIERCED

Prophecy:

…Then they will look on Me whom they pierced (Zechariah 12:10).

Fulfillment:

But one of the soldiers pierced His side with a spear, and immediately blood and water came out (John 19:34).

18. THE LAND DARKENED

Prophecy:

"And it shall come to pass in that day," says the Lord God, "that I will make the sun go down at noon, and I will darken the earth in broad daylight" (Amos 8:9).

Fulfillment:

Now from the sixth hour until the night hour there was darkness over all the land (Matthew 27:45).

The above prophecy and fulfillment speaks of darkness covering the Earth at the time Jesus was hanging on the cross. This presents a real problem for scientists and critics because Jesus was crucified at the time of Passover, which occurs during the full moon stage. You can't have a full moon and an eclipse happening at the same time because an eclipse occurs when the moon stands between the Earth and the sun. Still, the Bible says there was darkness over the Earth for about three hours during the time Jesus hung on the cross. This appears clearly contradictory to science and could not happen unless God miraculously suspended the laws of nature. However, that appears to be precisely what took place, and the event was documented by two non-biblical ancient historians. In his history of the Eastern Mediterranean (AD 52), Thallus, a Samaritan historian who lived in Rome in the first century AD wrote about the darkness that occurred during the crucifixion of Christ. He concluded that it appeared to be an eclipse of the sun, although it should not have happened during the time of the Passover.

Historian Phlegon of Tralles was quoted by church historian Eusebuis of Caesarea (AD 264-340) as saying that during AD 32/33, an eclipse of the sun occurred at the sixth hour, turning the day into darkness. Although logistically an eclipse of the sun should not have occurred during the time Jesus was crucified, its documentation by ancient historians confirms the biblical account.

19. THE EXACT YEAR OF HIS DEATH

Prophecy:

Seventy 'sevens' are decreed for your people and your holy city...Know therefore and understand this: from the issuing of the decree to restore and rebuild Jerusalem until the Messiah the Prince, there shall be seven weeks and sixty-two weeks...After sixty-two weeks the Messiah shall be cut off... And the people of the ruler who is to come shall destroy the city and the sanctuary... Then he shall confirm a covenant with many for one week... (Daniel 9:24-27).

Fulfillment:

This prophecy is known as *Daniel's 70 weeks prophecy*. Biblical scholars agree the interpretation of the word *week* represents seven years. Seven sets of seven (forty-nine years) added to sixty-two sets of seven (434 years) gives us a total of 483 years. God revealed to Daniel that 483 years would pass between the decree to rebuild Jerusalem and the Messiah's death.

According to prophecy expert Mark Hitchcock,

> When we calculate the span of time from the decree to rebuild and restore Jerusalem (on March 5, 444 B.C.) until the coming of Messiah as Irsael's Prince (on March 30, A.D. 33) we come up with a total of 173,880 days. Jesus had to be born in time to be an adult in A.D. 33. This prophecy pinpoints the time of His appearance to within one generation.[43]

20. STRUCK AND SPIT UPON

Prophecy:

I gave My back to those who struck Me, and My cheeks to those who plucked out the beard. I did not hide My face from shame and spitting (Isaiah 50:6).

Fulfillment:

Then they spat in His face and beat Him; and others struck Him with the palms of their hands (Matthew 26:67).

---

21. JOHN THE BAPTIST PRECEDING HIM

Prophecy:

A voice of one crying in the wilderness: "Prepare the way of the Lord; make straight in the desert a highway for our God" (Isaiah 40:3).

See I will send My messenger, who will prepare the way before Me. Then suddenly the Lord you are seeking will come to His temple; the messenger of the covenant whom you desire will come (Malachi 3:1 NIV).

Fulfillment:

John the Baptist came preaching in the wilderness of Judea, and saying, "Repent, for the kingdom of heaven is at hand" (Matthew 3:1-2).

From the non-biblical historians such as Josephus, we know that John the Baptist and Jesus were contemporaries of one another.

22. HE PRAYED FOR HIS ACCUSERS

Prophecy:

Therefore I will divide Him a portion with the great, and He shall divide the spoil with the strong, because He poured out His soul unto death, and He was numbered with the transgressors, and He bore the sin of many, ***and made intercession for the transgressors*** (Isaiah 53:12).

Fulfillment:

Then Jesus said, "Father, forgive them, for they do not know what they do" (Luke 23:34).

23. HE WAS CRUCIFIED WITH COMMON CRIMINALS

Prophecy:

> *Therefore I will divide Him a portion with the great, and He shall divide the spoil with the strong, because He poured out His soul unto death,* ***and He was numbered with the transgressors,*** *and He bore the sin of many, and made intercession for the transgressors* (Isaiah 53:12).

Fulfillment:

> *And when they had come to the place called Calvary, there they crucified Him, and the criminals, one on the right hand and the other on the left* (Luke 23:33).

As I stated earlier, Jesus fulfilled more than one hundred prophecies. Professor and statistician Peter W. Stoner, in an analysis reviewed by the American Scientific Affiliation, states the probability of just eight of these prophecies being fulfilled in one person is 1 in 10 to the 17th power. That's 1 in 100,000,000,000,000,000.[44] Think of it this way: Out of all the people who have ever lived on Earth from the beginning of time, estimates of about 25 to 30 billion, Jesus is *the* lone individual to fulfill every single one of the Messianic prophecies.

CONCLUSION

Though this chapter was lengthy, its contents are critical. From observing the facts in these six areas—Unity of Biblical Writings, Historical Accuracy, Archeological Evidence, Scientific Discoveries, Fulfilled Historical Prophecy, and Fulfilled Messianic Prophecy, we can plainly see how utterly *sane* it is to conclude that the Bible is God's Word and Jesus Christ is the Messiah. To refuse to acknowledge the living God and Christ, to me, is quite *insane.*

Of course, this chapter only touched on these particular facts. There are many more evidences for the faith and exhaustive resources on the subject. At the end of this book, I've compiled a list of some additional resources to check out.

> *But sanctify the Lord God in your hearts,* **and always be ready to give a defense to everyone who asks you a reason for the hope that is in you***, with meekness and fear* (1 Peter 3:15).

> *In the beginning was the Word, and the Word was with God, and the Word was God* (John 1:1).

Chapter 8

WHEN BAD THINGS HAPPEN AND EVIL APPEARS TO TRIUMPH

Outside of the resurrection of Jesus, I do not know of any other hope for the world. —Konrad Adenauer, Former Chancellor of West Germany, imprisoned by Adolf Hitler for opposing the Nazi regime

Not long ago, I watched a television interview with one of the world's leading scientists. Well mannered and pleasant, the scientist was not at all vindictive toward people of faith. She had come to the conclusion that science was not a hindrance to faith in God and that it often supported such faith. As she was making her point, however, she nonchalantly mentioned that she was an atheist. The interviewer, somewhat surprised, said, "Hold on a second. Let's go back to what I thought you just said. Did you say that you were an atheist?"

"Yes, that is correct," she responded politely.

"You're telling us that science lends support to God, and yet you are an atheist? That doesn't make sense."

The scientist's next response was honest and revealing. "Oh, I'm not an atheist because of science," she said. "I'm an atheist because of all the evil and suffering in the world. I can't imagine a God that would allow the Holocaust, war, and the torture and starvation of millions of innocent people. If God is a God of love," she continued, "He wouldn't allow that. He would step in and put a stop to it."

A sad expression fell across her face, as if she had some deep, unfulfilled longing in her heart for something more. "If anything," she said, "science gives me some hope that there may be a God. I would like to believe, but I just can't. Faith is a gift I would love to have." The woman was simply being honest, and my heart went out to her.

Charles Templeton, one of the world's most popular agnostics, said what finally convinced him to become an agnostic was the fact that God didn't send rain. *Life* magazine was doing a story on a devastating drought in northern Africa, and on the cover was a picture of a woman holding her dead child. Templeton said,

> She was holding her dead baby in her arms and looking up to heaven with the most forlorn expression. I looked at it and thought, "Is it possible to believe that there is a loving or caring Creator when all this woman needed was rain?" How could a loving God do this to that woman? Who runs the rain? I don't; you don't. He does—or that's what I thought. But when I saw that photograph, I immediately knew it is not possible for this to happen and for there to be a loving God. There is no way. Who else but a fiend could destroy a baby and virtually kill its mother with agony—when all that was needed was rain?[1]

On September 11, 2001, many good people, some with children and spouses and dreams, woke up and got dressed for their jobs at the World Trade Center. Perhaps they watched the morning news as they ate their bagel or grabbed a breakfast bar before they hurried out the door. Some frantically pulled their kids together just in time to catch the school bus. Others pecked their better halves on the cheek, wishing them a good day. But none had a clue that later that day some of them would be jumping out of windows to their deaths below or would be crushed by the collapsing twin towers. You saw the horrific images. They're tragic. They're unthinkable. We don't like to look at them because our minds can't comprehend such evil, such suffering. Yet it's reality. It happened.

And who among us has not reflected in sadness over images of emancipated Holocaust victims, wasted and withered, their bony faces blank and numb with disbelief as they were being herded into railroad cars like livestock being shipped off to slaughter, their dead bodies then tossed into massive piles and burned like refuse. Seeing such awfulness makes any honest observer want to scream, "God! Where were You? How could You have allowed this? Could You not see what was happening?" The Greek philosopher Epicurus (341-270 BC) once asked,

> Is [God] willing to prevent evil, but unable to do so? Then he is impotent. Is he able but unwilling? Then [God] is malevolent. Is he both willing and able? Whence, then is evil?[2]

On the surface, Epicurus' questions may seem unanswerable, and in all fairness to atheists and agnostics, their argument does seem to have some credibility. If God is so good, if He is real, then why does He seem so absent in the face of unspeakable evil and suffering? Why didn't God send rain? Why did three thousand innocent people die on September 11? Why did millions get slaughtered in the Holocaust? What about earthquakes, tornadoes, hurricanes, and tsunamis? Why is my son deaf? Why do bad things happen to good people, and why does evil appear to triumph?

As believers, it's all too easy to talk about evil and unfortunate events by offering cliché, often shallow-sounding religious answers until tragedy strikes us personally. As I write this chapter, one of my daughter's friends was tragically killed in an automobile accident. A man in a jacked-up pickup truck was going over 90 mph in a curvy 45 mph zone! The kid never knew what hit him. One moment he was planning for the homecoming dance; the next moment his parents were planning his funeral. Just sixteen-years-old, he was a warm-hearted gentleman. Everybody loved him, and his life was just beginning.

Now, try to imagine that you have the unthinkable task of explaining to these parents why God allowed this horrible tragedy. Believe me; I know what it's like because I've talked to hurting people following tragic circumstances. They were desperate for answers, clinging to what threads of faith they had left. And though we can surely experience God's supernatural peace and comfort during times like these, there are no great, wonderful answers that will erase the pain and loss of such events. I've learned that the time to discuss theology is not when people are in the grip of deep grief. Ultimately, it takes the healing work of the Holy Spirit to break through their pain and bring comfort. Ironically though, an understanding of sound theology is what is needed to sustain long-term healing and faith.

There are several key theological truths regarding the problem of evil and suffering in the world that have brought me great personal comfort and have actually enhanced my faith while in the midst of some of my life's greatest difficulties. Based on sound reasoning, these truths have helped keep me *sane* amidst apparent *insanity*. As we address these truths in the rest of this chapter, keep in mind, they work only after embracing what we've concluded up to this point. That is:

- God is real and personally involved in our lives.

- Jesus was God in the flesh. He is who He says He is.

- The Bible is a supernatural book, inspired by God. It is the Word of God.

- There are unseen spirit forces that we do battle against.

TRUTH #1. THE BIBLE'S UTTER HONESTY ABOUT LIFE

As strange as it may seem, the Bible's utter honesty about life and this world gives me great comfort when coming to terms with the unanswerable *whys* of life. The Word of God never denies that life is often hard and bad stuff happens—that there is unspeakable evil in the world and quite frequently it's the righteous who suffer because of it. The Bible pulls no punches and doesn't whitewash a thing. It tells it exactly like it is. From Genesis to Revelation, the Bible is chock-full of examples. Below are just a few.

The very first family was about as dysfunctional as you can get. Early on, evil got the upper hand when Cain murdered his brother, Abel, who may I remind you, was doing all the right things, following God's way. The good guy got the ax, and people have been killing each other ever since (see Gen. 4). Often it is the righteous who suffer from the hand of the wicked. I'm reminded of the massacre at Columbine High School in 1999, where several noted Christians like Cassie Bernall, Valeen Schnurr, and Rachel Scott were shot in cold blood when the gunmen asked them if they believed in God. As it was with Abel, there was no divine intervention to stop it.

Joseph did the right thing by *not* sleeping with Potiphar's wife, and you see where that got him! She was so angry at Joseph for his refusal of her sexual advances that she falsely accused him of attempted rape. No one stepped up to Joseph's defense. Everyone abandoned him, and it appeared God did, too. He was thrown into prison for around fourteen years! And don't forget, before the ordeal with Potiphar's wife, he was sold into slavery by his loving brothers who originally wanted to kill him (see Gen. 37–44).

Elijah the prophet did scores of mighty miracles and was eventually taken up to Heaven in a whirlwind (see 2 Kings 2:11). His protégé Elisha did twice as many miracles as he did, but in the end suffered and died from a terminal illness. After a life of following God and seeing all those miracles, Elisha didn't get one for himself (see 2 Kings 13:14).

Uriah was a faithful soldier who bravely went to battle to fight for his beloved King David. While he was on the front lines doing his duty, however, the king was at home doing his wife! David then had Uriah murdered on the battlefield to cover his sin (see 2 Sam. 11–12). What a reward for faithful service! So much for justice and honor in the world.

We all know about Job. He was a righteous man, yet he suffered through thieves who stole his wealth, wildfires that burned his fields, and a tornado that killed his children. Then he broke out in boils. As added torture, God allowed his nagging wife to hang around (see Job 1–2). Do things like that happen today? You bet they do. I know a woman who lost both of her Christian parents in a tornado. Siran Stacy, a committed Christ-follower, minister, and former football standout at the University of Alabama lost his wife and four children at once when their vehicle was struck by a drunk driver. Tears stream down people's faces and lives are changed when Siran tells his story of God's faithfulness through it all. But, still, it happened.

Consider John the Baptist. After living off of locust and honey in the wilderness, preaching and preparing the way for the coming Messiah, he finally saw Jesus face-to-face and even baptized Him in the Jordan River. John then witnessed the Holy Spirit descend upon Jesus in the form of a dove. One of the next statements John uttered was, *"He must increase, but I must decrease"* (John 3:30). How many loyal Christ-followers have quoted that one? John, however, didn't realize how literal and prophetic his statement was. Now fast forward a bit. John is in prison, about to be beheaded. It seemed that Jesus wasn't setting up His earthly kingdom like John had imagined. Death by beheading was certainly not what he had expected, especially since the Messiah was now here on Earth. Stuck in that cold, dark jail cell facing execution, John began to have some doubts, so he sent two messengers to ask Jesus if He really was the Messiah or should they look for another (see Matt. 11:2). Think about that for a moment. Really, John? After everything you'd witnessed? Yet, here's this great man of God in prison doubting so much that he's not even sure who Jesus is! Amazing! The dark dungeons of life will do that to us sometimes.

Then after John the Baptist's messengers caught up with Jesus, this is what Jesus said.

> *Go and tell John the things which you hear and see: The blind see and the lame walk; the lepers are cleansed and the deaf hear; the dead are raised up and the poor have the gospel preached to them. And blessed is he who is not offended because of Me* (Matthew 11:4-6).

Jesus gave John Scripture from Isaiah (see Isa. 29:18; 35:4-6; 61:1), and He knew that John might be offended. John didn't get miraculously delivered from prison, and his head ultimately rolled. John had to trust in the Word of God by faith just like the rest of us. At first glance, it appeared that Jesus didn't show the least bit of concern for John's welfare. He didn't even visit John. I'm quite certain that John the Baptist felt the cold silence of God and wondered why. Why would Jesus let him lose his head, but raise Lazarus? Did He love Lazarus more? Was John lacking in faith? I don't think so. It's possible to struggle with doubt and still have faith. Earlier Jesus had said, *"Assuredly, I say to you, among those born of women there has not risen one greater than John the Baptist..."* (Matt. 11:11). That's a pretty heavy compliment coming from Jesus. Sometimes God does not rescue us, and as with John the Baptist, He gives no explanation.

The eleventh chapter of Hebrews is the famous *faith* chapter. In it we are told what faith is and then given a list of men and women who were great in faith. We are told about Noah who, in faith, obeyed God and was supernaturally delivered from the Flood and about Sarah, who received the miracle baby, Isaac, though she was much too old. Hebrews goes on to say that they:

> *...through faith subdued kingdoms, worked righteousness, obtained promises, stopped the mouths of lions, quenched the violence of fire, escaped the edge of the sword, out of weakness were made strong, became valiant in battle, turned to flight the armies of the aliens. Women received their dead raised to life again* (Hebrews 11:33-35).

This is pretty awesome stuff, right? God is a God of miracles! I can do all things in Christ! We have the victory! Now, let's get out there and move that mountain! Rah! Rah! But before we launch our attack, we should read a bit further.

> *Still others had trial of mockings and scourgings, yes, and of chains and imprisonment. They were stoned, they were sawn in two, were tempted, were slain with the sword. They wandered about in sheepskin and goatskins, being destitute, afflicted, tormented...* (Hebrews 11:36-37).

What? Sawn in two? Slain with the sword? Tormented and destitute? Afflicted? How could God allow such things? But He did, and it's all right there written in Scripture.

The apostle Paul said in First Corinthians 15:19, *"If in this life only we have hope in Christ, we are of all men the most pitiable."* Why did Paul make such a statement? It was because life for him was pretty tough down here, especially after he became a Christ-follower. Paul continued in Second Corinthians 1:8-9, *"...We were burdened beyond measure, above strength, so that we despaired even of life. Yes, we had the sentence of death in ourselves..."* Burdened beyond measure? Despaired? I thought people of faith didn't despair? Paul surely did, and he had faith. He'd seen the risen Christ firsthand on the road to Damascus. Yet he still despaired. Even though Paul was a believer, he saw some rough times.

> *From the Jews five times I received forty stripes minus one. Three times I was beaten with rods; once I was stoned; three times I was shipwrecked; a night and a day I have been in the deep; in journeys often, in perils of waters, in perils of robbers, in perils of my own countrymen, in perils of the Gentiles, in perils in the city, in perils in the wilderness, in perils in the sea, in perils among false brethren; in weariness and toil, in sleeplessness often, in hunger and thirst, in fastings often, in cold and nakedness—besides the other things, what comes upon me daily...* (2 Corinthians 11:24-28).

No, Paul didn't have an easy life, but he still had peace and contentment. *"Not that I speak in regard to need, for I have learned in whatever state I am, to be **content"*** (Phil. 4:11). Paul could say that because he understood this world was fallen and was not his ultimate home.

Yes, the Bible is utterly honest. It even addresses unfortunate accidents. In Luke 13:4, when a tower collapsed and killed eighteen people, Jesus declared that the ones who perished were merely innocent victims.

> *What about those eighteen people in Siloam who were killed when the tower fell on them? Do you suppose this proves that they were worse than all the other people living in Jerusalem? No indeed...* (Luke 13:4-5 GNT).

Jesus said point blank, *"In the world you will have tribulation..."* (John 16:33). This *is* a promise. Needless to say, it's not a promise we like to quote very often. *Webster* defines *tribulation* as "misfortune, trials, suffering, pain, distress, trouble, and problems." Jesus wasn't being a pessimist. He was being honest. He was being a realist. Yet, Jesus also said in the same verse, *"...Be of good cheer, I have overcome the world."* We'll talk more about that a little later in the chapter. The point I want to stress now is that the Bible never attempts to pull the wool over our eyes. It doesn't sugarcoat things or try to cover for the fact that bad stuff sometimes happens. Biblical scholar N.T. Wright put it this way,

> [The Bible] never tries to give us the sort of picture the philosophers want, that of a static world order with everything explained tidily...What we are offered instead is stranger and more mysterious: a narrative of God's project of justice within a world of injustice...[3]

As strange as it may sound, the fact that the Bible displays life laid out in all its rawness, injustice, and pain gives me great comfort. For me, the Bible's utter honesty is just one more piece of evidence that validates the Christian faith. Why? Because humans never could have thought it up—the raw state of the human condition and its need for redemption. Former atheist C.S. Lewis expounded on this idea in his book *Mere Christianity*:

> Reality, in fact, is usually something you could not have guessed. That is one of the reasons I believe Christianity. It is a religion you could not have guessed. If it offered us just the kind of universe we had always expected, I should feel we were making it up. But, in fact, it is not the sort of thing anyone would have made up. It has just that queer twist about it that real things have…What is the problem? A universe that contains much that is obviously bad and apparently meaningless, but containing creatures like ourselves who know that it is bad and meaningless.[4]

We get upset when we see evil and suffering in the world and rightly so, but the Bible, God's Word, clearly said it would happen. God says it, and we know experientially that it is true. The Bible also doesn't deny the reality of the horrors and ravages of war.

> *And Jesus, answering them, began to say: "…when you hear of wars and rumors of wars, do not be troubled; for such things must happen, but the end is not yet. For nation will rise against nation, and kingdom against kingdom. And there will be earthquakes in various places, and there will be famines and troubles…"* (Mark 13:5-9).

Wars, famines, and earthquakes (natural disasters) all have several things in common—death, destruction, suffering, and heartache. Jesus, God in the flesh, said it would happen. So why are we so surprised when it does?

My first response to the Holocaust and 9/11 victims and the woman on the cover of *Life* magazine holding her dead baby is that we live in a fallen and broken world, where bad things sometimes happen, and God said it would be this way. However, God doesn't just leave us there. There is hope.

TRUTH #2. BELIEVE IT OR NOT, EVIL AND SUFFERING EXIST BECAUSE OF LOVE

So why doesn't God, as the scientist said, "Just step in and put a stop to it?" The imminent answer is: He has, and He's not finished yet. When God created the universe out of nothing, the apex of this creation was humanity. Unlike the rest of nature, God created people in His own image. To bear God's image refers in part to the ability to reason, to create, to be self-aware, to have regard for others, and to give and receive love. It also speaks of free will, to the extent that we can have it. I'm well aware of the debate between free will and God's absolute sovereignty. I am certainly no scholar, but I have studied quite extensively and reached a conclusion that makes the most rational sense to me and to many scholars as well. Yes, God is sovereign (in ultimate control over everything, even our wills), but within His sovereignty, He allows a certain amount of free will to humankind in order to accomplish His plan for this particular creation and time continuum. God is outside of time and is so big and beyond our comprehension that He is able to extend free will to humankind while at the same time still knowing what we are going to choose. This is how God can work "all" things, even "bad" things, for good.

We are called to a partnership with our Creator. Nowhere is this more evident than in prayer. Throughout Scripture, we are continually exhorted to pray expectantly, as if our prayers actually help create outcomes. Consider the following sample of Scriptures on prayer: *"...In whom we trust that He will still deliver us, you also **helping together in prayer** for us..."* (2 Cor. 1:10-11). *"...Men always ought to pray and not lose heart..."* (Luke 18:1). *"...For he who comes to God must believe that He is, and that He is a **rewarder of those who diligently seek** Him"* (Heb. 11:6). *"For this reason we also...do not cease to pray for you..."* (Col. 1:9). *"Continue earnestly in prayer, being vigilant in it..."* (Col. 4:2). *"Epaphras...[is]always laboring fervently for you in prayers..."* (Col. 4:12). *"...The effective, fervent* *prayer of a righteous man avails much…"* (James 5:16). These are just a few of the multitudes of passages on prayer.

Clearly, we are called to pray and expect answers. The book you are reading is full of testimonies of those who've had dramatic answers to prayer. This is not a study on prayer, but a point on God's sovereignty and yet people's role as free moral agents. If we had no free will, why even pray? Prayer is a calling to partnership with the Divine. Does God know what we need before we pray? Of course He does. Does God need us to pray to move on our behalf? The answer is "no." Why pray then? We pray because we are commanded to pray and to pray expectantly. Prayer is a mystery that we will not ultimately understand until we are in Heaven. The same is true with the balance of human free will and God's sovereignty. We will know completely when we are in His presence, but while on this Earth, we are enabled to make choices that affect outcomes, some good and some bad. The man driving the jacked up truck that hit my daughter's friend was exercising his free will. God could have stepped in and manipulated his driving, but He didn't. God is sovereign and has the ability to control all things, but that doesn't mean He does.

The ultimate reason for the creation of humankind was that God wanted beings who would willingly love Him and join Him in relationship and who would work with Him in partnership—now on Earth and eventually in Heaven. He wanted them to enjoy free will. To force love or a change of heart would pervert those beings into mere machines or animals with instinct. For true love to be possible, there must be freedom of choice. In order to choose to love, we must likewise be able to choose *not* to love. Some will choose love and some evil. Some who choose evil are responsible for the pain and suffering of others. Cain chose to disobey God's order and out of jealousy murdered Abel. There cannot be a positive without a negative. It's impossible. God knew that in order to endow human beings with free will, capable of reciprocal love, evil would also have to exist; therefore, suffering and injustice would exist as evil's natural by-products.

The ultimate choice in the garden, Adam and Eve's decision to disobey God's command and eat of the tree of life, was a clear example of exercising free will. Did God know what they were going to do? Of course, but it was worth the risk to create the ultimate. God's plan of redemption was already in place. Satan's forces are set on stopping that plan. God could have stepped in, exercised His authority, and put a stop to evil and suffering. But at what cost? It would have cost us our free will and the ability to love freely. The truth is, love is messy. When we get close to people, we see both their good points and their bad points. Wherever there is true love, there is always risk and the possibility of getting hurt. The same holds true with love on a much grander scale. God loved us so much that He gave us free will to choose whether we would love Him in return. God draws us by His Spirit, by grace. We can't even respond without that, but we still must choose. I can choose, but my bent is still toward the flesh. If He took away evil and suffering, He would have to take away from us that choice. C.S. Lewis wrote the following about free will:

> If a thing is free to be good it is also free to be bad. And free will is what has made evil possible. Why, then, did God give them free will? Because free will, though it makes evil possible, is also the only thing that makes possible any love or goodness or joy worth having. A world of automata—of creatures that worked like machines—would hardly be worth creating. The happiness which God designs for His higher creatures is the happiness of being freely, voluntarily united to Him and to each other in an ecstasy of love and delight compared with which the most rapturous love between a man and a woman on this earth is mere milk and water. And for that they must be free.[5]

God evidently thought creating beings capable of love and free will was worth the risk and the price. I like the way John Eldredge described it in his book *Epic:*

> *God gives us the freedom to reject him.* He gives to each of us a will of our own. Good grief, why?…He knows how we will use our freedom, what misery and suffering, what hell will be unleashed on earth because of our choices. Why? Is he out of his mind?
>
> The answer is as simple and staggering as this: if you want a world where love is real, you must allow each person the freedom to choose…Any parent or lover knows this: love is chosen. You cannot, in the end, force anyone to love you.
>
> So if you are writing a story where love is the meaning, where love is the highest and best of all, where love is the point, then you have to allow each person a choice. You have to allow freedom. You cannot force love. God gives us the dignity of freedom, to choose for or against him.[6]

In his book *Disappointment with God,* Philip Yancey put it another way:

> Power can do everything but the most important thing: it *cannot control love*…In a concentration camp, the guards possess almost unlimited power. By applying force, they can make you renounce your God, curse your family, work without pay, eat human excrement, kill and then bury your closest friend or even your own mother. All this is within their power. Only one thing is not: they cannot force you to love them. This fact may help explain why God sometimes seems shy to use his power. He created us to love him, but his most impressive displays of miracles—the kind we may secretly long for—do nothing to foster that love. As Douglas John Hall has put it, "God's problem is not that God is not

able to do certain things. God's problem is that God loves. Love complicates the life of God as it complicates every life."[7]

Even Harvard University and Senior Smithsonian astronomer Dr. Owen Gingerich thinks this idea makes sense.

> I would prefer to accept a universe created with intention and purpose by a loving God, and perhaps created with just enough freedom that conscience and responsibility are part of the mix. They may even be part of the reason that pain and suffering are also present in a world with its own peculiar integrity. This, for me, is God's universe.[8]

To answer the scientist at the beginning of this chapter: God allows evil to exist in the world now because of His love for us and because His work is not yet finished. One day, however, it will be finished, and God will step in and put a complete and final stop to all evil and suffering. In fact, He already has begun the process. Hebrews 2:8 explains, *"...He put all in subjection under him, He left nothing that is not put under him. **But now we do not yet see all things put under him**."* In other words, evil and suffering have not been done away with yet, but one day they will be.

God did something amazing and radical. In the midst of all this pain and sin, He didn't just point out our dilemma as a species, but He did something about it. God became one of us and entered into our sufferings. In all other religions, people have to jump through a thousand hoops to get to God, but in Christianity, God came down to us. God feels our pain. How do I know? I know because of the Cross. Jesus knows what it is like to suffer. He experienced His own suffering. He wept at the news of His friend Lazarus' death. He certainly knew injustice and betrayal. His own disciples abandoned Him in His darkest hour. In the garden, Jesus begged the Father to somehow let Him forgo the Cross. But the Father said, "No."

And when Jesus died on the cross, He experienced suffering and pain, both physical and emotional, to its utter fullness. The good news is that all that suffering was nailed to the cross with Him, and when He rose from the grave, He left it there. After His resurrection, He sent the Holy Spirit, God's Spirit, to be a very relevant Comforter to us. That's why Jeremiah could write, *"O Lord, my strength and my fortress, my refuge in times of distress"* (Jer. 16:19 NIV). We can run to God in times of distress because He knows how we feel. *"Blessed be the God and Father of our Lord Jesus Christ, the Father of mercies and God of all comfort, who comforts us in all our tribulation…"* (2 Cor. 1:3-4). If we never had tribulation, there would be no need for comfort.

TRUTH #3. WE MUST RESPOND AS JESUS RESPONDED

It seems to me that, as believers, the proper response to evil and suffering is to examine how Christ Himself responded to it and then follow suit. Whenever Christ, who was God incarnate, came face-to-face with suffering or evil, He never felt the need to explain it or apologize for it. He simply dealt with it.

On one occasion in the Gospels, a number of Galileans had been cruelly murdered by Pilate while they were in the act of making their sacrifices to God. This was a particularly monstrous act of evil committed by a monster of a man. Matthew Henry's commentary indicates that these Galileans, when they offered their animal sacrifices, had unintentionally broken some Roman regulation. As a result, Pilate had them slaughtered. It was a bloodbath, and innocent people were murdered.

A group of Pharisees, questioning why God had allowed this to happen, felt surely it was due to some sin the Galileans had committed. They also saw it as an opportunity to trap Jesus with a trick question. But Jesus answered, *"Do you think that these Galileans were worse sinners than all the other Galileans because they suffered this way?*

I tell you, no" (Luke 13:2-3 NIV). In essence, Jesus was saying that everyone is sinful and in need of God. Everyone misses the mark of perfection, and these Galileans didn't do anything especially wrong to cause this terrible suffering to befall them. It was a result of living in a fallen, sin-inundated world where evil flourishes. The Galileans made a mistake, broke some rules, and paid the ultimate price.

Touching on the tower incident again, in order to illustrate His point further, Jesus brought up another event, an unfortunate accident: *"Or those eighteen who died when the tower in Siloam fell on them—do you think they were more guilty than all the others living in Jerusalem? I tell you, no* (Luke 13:4-5 NIV). Jesus didn't apologize for the existence of evil or for the bad things that happen. Those things were not His focus. His attention was always on His purpose, which was to breathe new life into dead situations and to bring life to people who were spiritually dead. After Jesus addressed the Siloam accident, He told the Pharisees, *"But unless you repent, you too will all perish"* (Luke 13:5). Jesus was being strong here because He knew the hardness of the Pharisees' hearts. But He was also extending an invitation to spiritual rebirth. Jesus was asserting to them that, yes, bad things happen, and we are all under the curse of sin. He was also imploring them to recognize that, unless each of us repents and receives new life, we will remain under sin's curse. Jesus was more eager to change and redeem lives than He was to explain why evil, tragic things happened in those lives.

GOD'S STRATEGY

God's strategy for dealing with evil was to send His Son into the middle of it and to defeat it, to break the power of sin in the world, and to reconcile people to Himself through Jesus. When Jesus hung on that cross and died, it appeared that evil had triumphed and Satan had won. But then, out of the ashes of defeat, God manifested His power, and Christ rose from the grave, conquering the power of evil and death once and for all.

Yes evil and suffering exist, but God's work is not yet finished, and He calls us to share in His redemptive work. The apostle Paul, who certainly knew firsthand the definition of suffering, exhorted us, *"Do not be overcome by evil, but overcome evil with good"* (Rom. 12:21).

God has commissioned us to carry out His work. Part of our mission is, through the Holy Spirit's power, to overcome evil with good and to partner with God in the creation of something good where evil now resides. Notice that I'm not saying there's a little bit of good in everything, even in evil, for which we should look. No. I'm talking about how God can take evil and by His power *transform* it into something good. There's a big difference.

Consider this: God's work as the Maker and Designer of the universe involved the creation of something out of nothing. Scientists, to this day, even with all the available technology, are unable to create one single molecule of matter. We can do wonders with the matter that already exists. We can reshape it, break it down, and change its form. But we are unable either to create it or destroy it. Scientists have yet to figure out exactly how matter came into existence. Just as God formed matter out of nothing in His creation of the universe, His role as Redeemer in our lives involves the creation of something good where formerly there was nothing good. This is why the Christ-follower can stand with confidence on Romans 8:28: *"And we know that in all things God works for the good of those who love Him."* (NIV) Notice the little word *all*. God is able to work good in *all* situations, even in those exceedingly painful circumstances in which the good is absent and evil seems to triumph. God can create something good where good doesn't exist.

Joseph, as we mentioned earlier, was a faithful and honorable man, but he was betrayed by his own brothers, sold into slavery, and falsely accused; he wound up in prison for about fourteen years. By all outward appearances, it seemed God had abandoned Joseph. Yet nothing could be farther from the truth. God was with Joseph every step of the way. In the end, when he was brought out of prison and promoted to the second highest in command of all Egypt, God used him to save millions of people and prosper Egypt during great famine. In the end, Joseph was able to say, *"But as for you, you **meant evil** against me; but God **meant** it for good, in order to bring it about as it is this day, to save many people alive"* (Gen. 50:20).

My friend, Pastor Malcolm Richard, oozes with the love of God. His life is dedicated to pouring life into others. Soft-spoken and grace-oriented, he knows how to encourage people, especially hurting people. Malcolm knows peace, but it's not because he doesn't know pain. About six years ago, his twenty-five-year-old son, Justin, committed suicide when he experienced depression as a side-effect from a certain medication. Devastated, Malcolm went though all the stages of grief. For a while he questioned God and was angry with God, but in the end, it is God's Spirit and reality that sustains him. "It still hurts," says Malcolm. "Only God's grace keeps me going. Justin's death is still touching lives and helping others. His death has certainly caused me to depend on Jesus more and love my family more than ever. It is not a ministry I ever wanted or desired, but almost every week God brings across my path parents who have lost a child. It is the greatest grief, and they need to know that somehow they can make it! Our new church, Journey Church, was birthed out of a vision to help people like Justin. The hurting, broken, addicted folks of society whom some in the church world often see as outcasts and unlovable, with their holier-than-thou attitudes—a church where it is okay to not be okay. Lives have already been saved and changed because of Justin's death. In that truth, I am thankful."

> *Blessed the God and Father of our Lord Jesus Christ, the Father of mercies and God of all comfort, who comforts us in all our tribulation, that we may be able to comfort those who are in any trouble, with the comfort with which we ourselves or comforted by God* (2 Corinthians 1:3-4).

TRUTH #4. WHEN THE WORST DAY OF OUR LIVES IS ACTUALLY THE BEST DAY OF OUR LIVES—AN ANGELIC ENCOUNTER AND AN ETERNAL VIEW OF SUFFERING

Paul said, *"If **in** this life only we have **hope in Christ**, we are of all men the most pitiable"* (1 Cor. 15:19). Paul made that statement for two basic reasons. #1) He was experiencing much pain and suffering in this life. #2) He had seen the risen Christ and took much comfort in the life to come. Paul knew this life is all about the next life—eternity.

There is pain, suffering, and corruption in this world, but God *is* dealing with it. One day He will bring it to an end. Now here's a radical thought. What if the worst day of our lives is actually the best day? What if what we see as tragedy is actually a wonderful experience to those who are in Christ?

Next, I want to tell you about my friend Bob Bell's incredible story. But before I do, it's necessary that I give you his background. Bob has been a Navy JAG officer/attorney handling cases for the United States Navy for thirty years. He also worked as a civilian trial lawyer representing numerous high profile insurance companies, including Lloyd's of London. Professional and highly educated, Bob graduated from Emory Law School, one of the top schools in the country. Bob is as solid as they come.

In addition, I know him personally and also know that he has absolutely no motive to concoct, embellish, or even reveal the details of his story. In fact, Bob would rather *not* tell his story at all because he's aware that many people will look at him with raised eyebrows, questioning his veracity. Yet he feels compelled to share his story because it brings hope and comfort to hurting people. It also shows us that God is real, knows each of us intimately, and is working in our lives even though we often cannot see or understand our circumstances. The following story is in Bob's own words:

BISCAYNE BOULEVARD, JULY 19

"Oh, God, he's going to hit us!" Muffin cried as an oncoming truck veered directly into our path. In the next instant, I heard a thunderous shout above us, followed almost simultaneously by a magnificent burst of light with a single beam shooting down toward Earth, both illuminating and enveloping everything around us. Racing down the beam of light with amazing speed was what appeared to be an ancient soldier, armed with a sword and wearing a military kilt that came down just below his knees. I was galvanized by this shocking, spectacular sight. Then, just as quickly as he appeared, he was gone. As hard as it was to comprehend, the entire electrifying episode happened in a split second while time seemed to be moving in slow-motion.

Snapping back to the grim reality of the speeding truck hurling toward us, I instinctively jerked our car slightly to the right so my side of the car would bear the brunt of the brutal crash that was coming. I wasn't trying to be a hero. I was terrified, but I hoped my desperate, split-second maneuver would spare the lives of my wife, Muffin, and of our two-and-a-half-year-old daughter, Elizabeth. I bravely braced for impact.

As the truck smashed into my side of the car, I momentarily saw the eyes of the other driver, glowing strangely red and evil. The truck rode up over the hood of our Toyota, its front tires crushing our windshield and obliterating our dashboard. Glass shards flew everywhere, embedding in my face and head. The force of the impact broke the metal frames of my eyeglasses, but the shatterproof lenses protected my eyes for an instant before the lenses dropped to the floor. Then a strange thing happened. The man in the ancient battle dress suddenly appeared again, coming between me and the truck, pushing it away from me with a super-human strength. I was absolutely amazed and awed and also gripped with instant gratitude that he was coming to the rescue. No mere man could do what he had just done. Then he disappeared again.

Stunned and dazed, I leaned over to check on Muffin. Even though she was unresponsive, I kissed her cheek and told her I loved her. I then told her goodbye in case one or both of us did not survive. I heard some sounds from Elizabeth, but I could not see into the other side of the back seat where she was in her car safety seat. It was dark, I did not have my glasses, and the roof of the car was collapsed on that side.

Suddenly, I was aware of someone talking to me through my open window. It was the driver of the truck, seemingly unharmed. He leaned in close to my face in the dark and asked loudly, "Is anyone alive in there?"

"Yes," I cried. "We need help."

"Don't worry," he yelled back, "you won't live long." With that, he ran away from the scene, leaving us to die.

In one frantic attempt, I struggled to get out of the car to go help Muffin and Elizabeth on the other side. Somehow, I managed to get out of the car. The effort caused me to collapse on the pavement close to the oncoming line of vehicles. As the headlights went by me in seemingly endless succession, I lay on my back in the road, drifting in and out of consciousness, yet with a dazed, general awareness of my surroundings. I was cold and shivering. Someone came and put something over me as I lay there to try to keep me warm and stop the shivering that was shaking me as I was losing consciousness. Then the curtain of death came down over my life, and I lost consciousness completely.

Immediately after I finally lost all consciousness at the scene of the wreck, I somehow saw my precious wife as her spirit separated from her physical body. Her new body glowed with radiant energy. Then I saw Elizabeth. She, too, had separated from her physical body and was playing around her mother. I realized at that moment, I, too, had separated from my physical body and was free of pain.

As we separated from our bodies, the ancient war- rior appeared again, coming to the rescue. This time, though, he was glowing with an even brighter aura of energy about him. I realized, finally, he must be an angel, although I did not know his name. For the first time, I noticed his military garb was colored in shades of white, including very light gold and beige, although the shades and colors were somewhat obscured by the glow of light surrounding him. The beam of light that appeared from the sky just before the impact was now like a stairway or escalator. That's the best way I can describe it. The angel started ascending the stairway toward Heaven. Muffin turned to follow him. When Elizabeth did not follow, Muffin turned around, looked at me and Elizabeth, and called her to come. Elizabeth lingered just a moment longer, still frolicking about, but she soon followed her mother as instructed.

I, too, started to follow both of them up the moving stairway so we could stay together, but the angel saw what I was doing and came back to me. "Stop!" he shouted, "Your time has not come yet. You still have work to be done on Earth." He stuck his hand in my chest and forcefully, but not violently, shoved me back down the stairway of light. It was then I saw Muffin kneel and bow in humble adoration when she reached the top of the stairway. She and Elizabeth soon disappeared out of sight as if going over a hill. There was a glow of light coming from the other side, along with sounds of music, celebration, and joy.

I was tremendously grateful they were in Heaven, but I was emotionally shattered that I was not going there with them. "Why can't I die and be with my wife and daughter?" I frantically pleaded with the angel.

"If you choose to die when you can live," he counseled, "that would be a sin and could be held against you. It may not be advisable for you to choose to die when you can live, as you may face judgment in that condition." The angel also told me if I died, the man who killed my wife and daughter would get away with his crime. He told me this man had previously gotten away with many evil things and that God was ready to bring him to justice. I needed to live and be an eyewitness to his crime. If I lived, other witnesses would be discovered and would come forward to testify against this man.

I definitely did not want the man who killed my wife and daughter to go unpunished, but I certainly did not want to be separated from them either. There was no satisfactory solution to the situation. Earlier, while I was drifting in and out of consciousness lying on my back near my car, I heard the paramedics on the scene say every bone in my body was broken. "I don't want to live as an invalid, I would rather be dead," I argued angrily with the angel, attempting to change his action that was brutally blocking my path to my family.

"You will not have any broken bones," he promised. "You will be healed." He reached out with his sword and

touched my left arm at the elbow. I felt a surge of healing energy, fusing my bones together again. While I was
immensely grateful for his healing touch, I wondered
why he touched my left elbow when my entire right side
was badly injured. He told me for the healing energy to
be most effective it needed to enter my body through an
area that was whole. Apparently, my left elbow was one
area of my body that was not injured.

As I wrestled with issues of life and death with the angel,
the driver of the truck fled down the embankment of a
nearby canal, hiding in the bushes in the water…

Bob was hit by a drunk driver, his wife and daughter were
killed, he saw them go up into Heaven, and he was miraculously
healed. You could say he had one of those worst days. For his wife
and daughter, though it appeared to everyone else that it was the
worst day for them, they went into the very presence of God, which
I would think would be pretty good for a believer. The apostle Paul
said, *"We are confident, yes, **well pleased rather** to be absent from
the body and to be present with the Lord"* (2 Cor. 5:8). Bob's story
gets much more involved. The angel revealed several very specific
prophetic events that took years to come to pass, but did. To learn
more about Bob's story, see "People Behind the Stories" at the end
of the book.

CONCLUSION

How do we reconcile an almighty God with the pain and suffering and death in this world? I don't know that we will have a full
understanding of that until we meet our Creator, but I do know
that the Bible is God's Word, and it is honest about the struggles
and tragedies of this life. I find some comfort in the fact that Jesus
came into a world with pain and suffering and was subject to its
effects just as we are. He didn't change the natural order of things
on the Earth, which includes the ability to choose good or evil and

the acceptance of circumstances that occur as part of life. While I was writing this book, my pastor friend and author Richard Exley told me, "In the final analysis, the question of evil and the suffering it entails is not a riddle to be solved, but a mystery to be entrusted to the wisdom of God." I believe that is wise counsel.

We may not understand all things, but we can trust God to work all things, even evil and suffering, for good, though that good may not always be recognizable in this life. We ultimately must choose to believe that God is sovereign and that pain and suffering are a part of the reality of living on this Earth. I'm not being pessimistic. I'm being real. We live in a fallen world, but we that have Christ have hope and power.

> *And we know that all things work together for good to those who love God, to those who are the called according to His purpose* (Romans 8:28).

> *But we have this treasure in earthen vessels, that the excellence of the power may be of God and not of us. We are hard-pressed on every side, yet not crushed; we are perplexed, but not in despair; persecuted, but not forsaken; struck down, but not destroyed* (2 Corinthians 4:7-9).

> *Blessed are those who mourn, for they shall be comforted* (Matthew 5:4).

Chapter 9

WHAT SETS PEOPLE FREE

Faith is nothing other than believing God. —Nick Kalivoda[1]

Thus far in this book, we have observed some indisputable facts from science to archeology to miracles and powerful accounts of God moving in people's lives, all pointing to the absolute *sanity* of belief. But what would prevent someone from accepting this? As we discussed earlier, some profess atheism or unbelief due to suffering and evil in the world. For others, it could be due to disappointments, anger, grief, intellectualism, or how they were raised. People have many reasons for their seemingly impregnable stances for unbelief. Yet time and time again, I've witnessed the power of God smashing people's stony hearts and setting them free.

My friend Carol was an outspoken atheist who perceived herself as more intellectually superior than most people, especially Christians. Skeptical and highly critical of anyone who spoke on matters of faith, she often ridiculed them. To Carol, Christians were simply part of the gullible masses who fell prey to master manipulators of guilt and oppression. Not Carol though. She knew the facts of science and psychology. No way was she going to be duped. To most people who knew her, Carol was a hard, cynical, and unhappy person. But then something happened. Carol contracted colon cancer, and the prognosis wasn't good. She was given less than a year to live. Fighting hard against the dreaded disease, she did everything the doctors had recommended—diet, chemotherapy, radiation, and so forth—but in the end, her body didn't respond, and Carol began to waste away.

During this time, someone gave her a copy of my book *Desperate Dependence: When You Reach the End, God's Best Begins*. I'm quite sure that normally Carol would not have even considered reading it, but under these adverse circumstances, she did. One day I received a phone call from her. We lived in the same town, and a friend of mine had given her the book. She explained to me in a very matter-of-fact manner that she was dying and her time was short, that she had read my book and was wondering if I would consider doing her funeral service. Humbled by the request, I told her I would be honored, but would like to visit with her first. She welcomed the idea, and I saw it as an opportunity to share the Gospel with her. For the next few weeks, Carol and I visited on a regular basis. Before our first visit, however, I was warned by some about how hard and critical she was, for me to "not get my hopes up."

When I entered her home for my first visit, I was met by Carol's husband and grown daughter. Her daughter was soft spoken and friendly, but also an atheist. She'd flown in from out of state to care take. She was grateful I had come, but gave me the distinct impression that my purpose for being there was simply to help soothe her mother's transition, that it was all purely therapeutic. She was very polite, but didn't want to hear anything about God. Carol's husband, on the other hand, was a hardcore, religious zealot. I couldn't believe it and was amazed that the two were even married. *How could this be?* I remember thinking. Of the things I'd heard about Carol, not once was I told that her husband was this way. He was a rigid, legalistic know-it-all with little comprehension of God's grace. To him, God was angry and condemning, and His judgment was about to be released on humankind. Quickly, the situation began to make sense to me. Evidently, he had shoved his legalistic form of religion down Carol's throat for years, and she had resisted like a mad porcupine. If God was like him, she wanted no part. I couldn't say that I blamed her. On the other hand, Carol was looking for excuses *not* to believe, and her husband had given her plenty, as did many other religious people. They'd given her a stockpile of ammunition through the years to use against them that ranged from unethical behavior to hypocrisy to just plain stupidity. Carol's husband was sure that I was one of those apostate preachers who were "soft" on sin. I, on the other hand, questioned his work-based religiosity and whether he even knew Christ at all. In my experience, self-righteousness is the ugliest sin of all. The following quote from A.W. Tozer summed up my thoughts pretty well.

> The doctrine of justification by faith—a biblical truth, and a blessed relief from sterile legalism and unavailing self-effort—has in our time fallen into evil company and been interpreted by many in such a manner as actually to bar men from the knowledge of God.[2]

Carol's husband didn't want me to talk to her because he felt it was much too late. To him, she had sown her seeds of rebellion and now was reaping the harvest (I'm not kidding here). This guy needed Jesus to set him free just as much as his wife did! Oh, he had a ton of church rules and regulations, but his heart was far from God. As far as I could tell, there was no genuine relationship with Christ present.

Each time I went to visit, he would leave the house upon my entry. On that first visit, the daughter led me to the back bedroom where Carol lay. I sat at her bedside, and the two of us began our short-lived friendship. Carol told me that because she had read my book and had felt something reach out to her, she thought that maybe there was a God after all. She still wanted no part of religion, yet in the face of death, her once solid arguments against God began to wane. She knew there had to be more and was afraid of dying. Over the following weeks, as I opened God's Word and read to her,

I saw a transformation take place. As Carol began to *believe* and receive the simple truth of God's Word and His plan of redemption, I could see before my very eyes the weight she'd carried for so many years begin to lift. The once hard, skeptical shell of a person was now relaxed, almost ready to pass on. She had peace with God. God's Word was bearing witness in her spirit that it was truth. Of course, when I told her husband the good news, he refused to accept it because she had not bought in to his rigid religious system. But religious systems are not what set people free. What sets people free is simple faith and trust in what Jesus did at the Cross—believing God. At the funeral, I was able to comfort the family and friends with the fact that Carol had indeed trusted in Christ and was ready to meet her Creator, but her husband didn't accept it.

If Carol was so confident that there was no God, to the point of ridiculing other believers, if she was so certain that she was right, then why did she even call me? I believe she called me because, facing sure death, she began to think, *What if God is real and there is something beyond this life? If so, I'm about to find out. What do I have to lose if I'm wrong? Only my soul.* In her brokenness, Carol's stubborn rejection of God began to weaken, and she began to reconsider her basis for unbelief. She became much more honest with herself and eventually embraced the promises of God and the hope of believers. Many people who have spent their lives in adamant denial of God or in unbelief begin to question their viewpoints when they sense the nearness of death.

CREATED FOR ETERNITY

Whether people are atheists, agnostics, or just living outside of relationship with God, there is a vacuum within them that can only be filled by our Creator, God. Ecclesiastes 3:11 says, *"He has put eternity in their hearts."* That's quite a statement. It simply means humanity was created by God to live in fellowship with Him forever. It's the way we were fashioned. We can never find true peace of mind or become what we were designed to be outside of God's Spirit coming inside of us, reconciling us to Him. People can deny it, but that doesn't diminish the truth. To unbelievers, something will always be missing, regardless of what they do to fill the vacuum. As we get closer to death and it becomes obvious that we aren't going to live forever, the vacuum becomes more intense. That brings us to the other undeniable factor in this discussion. One hundred percent of us are going to die. Regardless of all the arguments and philosophical debates, we're all going to die. My friend Mike is a chaplain for a biker's club. They ride their big "Hogs" all over the country and meet other bikers at rallies. He has a tattoo on his forearm that reads *"One Breath Away."* Mike can tell story after story about the doors that tattoo has opened to speak to people about Christ. Someone will ask him what it means, and he says, "Hey man, regardless of who we are, we're all only one breath away from eternity." It gets their attention. Yet despite the fact that we are all just *"One Breath Away,"* most of us have become experts at pushing death out of our minds and living as though we are never going to die. Psalm 90:12 says, *"So teach us to number our days, that we may gain a heart of wisdom."* It is wise to understand that our days on this Earth are limited and, thus, to live accordingly. We can fight death, trying to hold on to this life as long as we can, but it's only delaying the inevitable. It *is* going to happen. We are all going to die.

Humanists and New Agers often talk about the great "circle" of life like death is this natural thing and dying is just completing everything. But if death is simply part of the great "circle" of life, why do we resist it so much? The reason we resist death the way we do is because we were not created for it. God created us with *"eternity"* in our hearts. People are supposed to live forever. Death is unnatural, a result of sin's curse. On this subject, Philip Yancey wrote:

> As for death, man responds to it even less like an animal. Nature treats death as a normal occurrence, the foundation of the all-important food chain. Only we humans react with shock and elaboration, as though we can't get used to the fact. We dress up our corpses in

new clothes, embalm them, and bury them in airtight coffins and concrete vaults to slow natural decay. We act out a stubborn reluctance to yield to this most powerful of life experiences. [This reaction] hints to another world. In a way unique to our species, we are not fully at home here. As a symptom of that fact, we feel stirrings toward something higher and more lasting.[3]

Many people boast of their certainty that there's no God, but when push comes to shove, when facing death, like Carol, their certainties become dubious. While I was writing this book, outspoken atheist Christopher Hitchens died at age 62. He spent his life arguing against God, but in the end, he still died, which to me kind of makes all of his arguments mute. I have no knowledge that he changed his view, but Hitchens is dead. I suppose he knows the truth now, and I say that with all compassion.

ATHEISM IS A DYING BREED

This brings me to another important point. Despite what the media and academia tells us, atheism is losing numbers in droves. Oh, some of the more militant will no doubt go on Amazon.com and rip me to shreds. That doesn't bother me though because I've seen too much of the truth, plus the statistics just don't support them, even among the most educated. Steven Waldman reported the following on NPR.

> Two surveys earlier this year—one in Harris, and one from Gallup—indicate that even supernatural religious beliefs are held not only by most Americans, but by the majority of well-educated Americans. Listen to the numbers—55% of people with post-graduate degrees (lawyers, doctors, dentists, and the like) believe in the devil. 53% believe in hell. 72% believe in miracles. Remember these are people with post-graduate educations. 78% of them believe in the survival of the soul

after death. 60% believe in the virgin birth. And 64% believe in the resurrection of Christ.[4]

According to another poll compiled by the *International Bulletin of Missionary Research,* as of mid-2011, there are an average of 80,000 new Christians added worldwide every twenty-four hours, but atheists *lose* about 300 every twenty-four hours. This survey and others like it reveal that the reports claiming Christianity is dying have been vastly over-stated.[5]

There are three main reasons why I believe atheism is a dying breed.

1. The evidence doesn't support it.

2. The longing for "eternal" things was placed in our hearts by God, and God is drawing us to Him.

3. We are all going to die, which means we have to deal with it, and that often prompts a re-evaluation of one's basis for unbelief.

My experience has been consistent with the above three points, particularly when people become broken. Brokenness is a good thing if it causes us to look to God. *"The Lord is near to those who have a **broken** heart, and saves such as have a **contrite** spirit"* (Ps. 34:18). *"…A **broken** and a **contrite** heart—these, O God, You will not despise"* (Ps. 51:17). Not all, but most people's rock-solid facades crack under the pressure of brokenness or the prospect of death.

JESUS BREATHES LIFE INTO DEAD SITUATIONS

We've seen from the numbers that atheism is a dying breed. I've witnessed those living in unbelief and the ultimate emptiness, void, and spiritual death it leads to. On the other hand, Jesus Christ breathes life into dead situations, into spiritually dead people. He can do it because He himself rose from the dead and is still very much alive. How else can you explain the startling transformations in the lives of believers throughout the centuries, beginning with Jesus' own disciples? According to history, all of the disciples except Judas and John (who was tortured) died a martyr's death. Also, Paul the apostle was martyred. Let me tell you about them.[6]

Bartholomew—AD 70 Armenia

For refusing to stop preaching the gospel of Christ, King Astyages of Armenia had Bartholomew beaten with rods, crucified, and skinned alive. Still conscious, he continued to exhort people to believe in Jesus. Finally, to prevent him from saying anything else, the king's men took an ax and cut off his head.

James the Less—AD 63 Jerusalem

While in prayer, James was beaten, stoned, and clubbed to death with a heavy stick.

Andrew—AD 66 Greece

Andrew the brother of Peter was crucified by the Roman Governor, Aegaeas. After the governor threatened to crucify him, Andrew answered, "If I were afraid of the death of the cross, I would not have preached about the majesty, honor, and glory of the cross."

Peter—AD 67 Jerusalem

After being sentenced to be crucified, Peter proclaimed that he was not worthy to be crucified in the same position as his Jesus and requested to be hung upside down on the cross.

John—AD 95 Patmos

John was tortured by being boiled in a basin of oil, but didn't die. He was forced to drink poison, but didn't die. He was banished to the island of Patmos to live alone in exile, where he wrote the Book of Revelation. Eventually, he was brought back where he died of old age.

Thomas—AD 70 Calamina, India

When Thomas preached the truth of Jesus to sun worshipers, the pagan priests were so angry that they thrust spears through his side.

James, son of Zebedee—AD 44 Jerusalem

The first of the twelve disciples to die for his faith, James, son of Zebedee, was beheaded by order of King Herod Agrippa I. The event is recorded in Acts 12:1-2.

Philip—AD 51 Heliopolis, Phrygia, Asia

Philip was whipped, thrown in prison, and later tied to a pillar and stoned to death.

Matthew—AD 66 Ethiopia

Matthew was nailed to the ground with short spears and then beheaded.

Jude, brother of James—AD 68 Persia

Because of his teachings, Jude was attacked and beaten to death with sticks and clubs.

Simon—AD 70 Syria

Simon was painfully tortured and then crucified by a governor in Syria.

Paul—AD 65 Rome

Paul was imprisoned and then beheaded by Nero for refusing to stop preaching the Gospel.

It's pretty consistent across the board. Every single one of them was tortured for Christ, refusing to recant, and that's not even counting Stephen, who was stoned to death for preaching Jesus (see Acts 7). What else is interesting is that all the disciples, save one, disappeared when Christ was facing his death. And Paul, who wasn't one of the original twelve, was a Jewish anti-Christ. We'll get to him later. But those first disciples of Christ were a bunch of cowards. They all split and were hiding out while Jesus was being crucified. So much for loyalty. When Jesus was arrested and being led away (you know the story), Peter was so afraid that he denied he knew Jesus three times and even cursed Him. Now all of a sudden, we see these same eleven cowards empowered with such boldness that every one of them laid down their lives in excruciatingly painful ways for the Christ they'd once denied. My question to you is "Why?" How could these guys make such a dramatic change in attitude? I think you know the answer. The apostles encountered the resurrected Christ firsthand. That is the only logical explanation.

People will occasionally die for something that they believe is true. But very few, if any, will die excruciatingly painful deaths for what they *know* is a lie. That would be *insane*. If what they were preaching was a lie, surely at least one of them would have cracked under the pain of torture. Peter Kreeft, professor of philosophy at Boston College and at the King's College in New York City, said,

> Why would the apostles lie?...Lies are always told for some selfish advantage. What advantage did the "conspirators" derive from their lie? They were hated, scorned, persecuted, excommunicated, imprisoned, tortured, exiled, crucified, boiled alive, roasted, beheaded, disemboweled, and fed to lions—hardly a list of perks!"[7]

Personally, I can hardly take it when I bump my "Funny Bone," so it seems inconceivable to me that not one of those guys recanted if what they were preaching was a lie. Remember, too, that we're not talking about fables here. These were actual, historically documented events that took place in real places with real people. These guys not only saw the risen Christ, but they were empowered by Him on the Day of Pentecost when the Holy Sprit came upon them. On the Day of Pentecost, only fifty days after the resurrection, these same cowards boldly addressed the crowd of thousands gathered in Jerusalem, specifically preaching that Christ had indeed risen. And they were so effective that some three thousand believed (see Acts 2). How is that possible?

The apostle Paul was another who died a martyr's death. He claimed to have encountered the risen Christ on the road to Damascus. He was heading there with the intent of shutting down and arresting some Christians when his party was overtaken by a blinding light in which Jesus revealed Himself (see Acts 9). After the encounter on the Damascus Road, Paul's life took a 180-degree turn. He went from being a comfortable, highly-educated, wealthy, successful Pharisee who persecuted Christians to, as we saw back in Chapter 8, being whipped with leather, beaten with rods, stoned, shipwrecked, robbed, sleeping in the wilderness, hungry, thirsty, cold, regularly imprisoned, and finally beheaded. It was all because he claimed to have seen the risen Jesus.

Again and again in his epistles, Paul, known formerly as Saul, states, *"Christ is risen from the dead."* When giving his defense before King Agrippa, Paul said,

> *...At midday, O king, along the road I saw a light from heaven, brighter than the sun, shining around me and those who journeyed with me. And when we all had fallen to the ground, I heard a voice speaking to me and saying in the Hebrew language, "Saul, Saul, why are you persecuting Me?..." So I said, "Who are You, Lord?" And He said, "I am Jesus, whom you are persecuting"...* (Acts 26:13-15).

Everywhere Paul went, he told his story. To the church at Corinth, Paul said,

> *...Christ died for our sins according to the Scriptures [Old Testament], and that He was buried, and that He rose again the third day according to the Scriptures, and that He was **seen by Cephas, then by the twelve.** After that He was **seen by over five hundred brethren at once,** of*

whom the greater part remain to the present, but some have fallen asleep. After that He was seen by James, then by all the apostles. Then last of all **He was seen by me also***...* (1 Corinthians 15:3-8).

Paul could have never made those statements, especially about the five hundred eyewitnesses, if they didn't actually exist. Most were still alive, and their stories could have been verified by anyone. John Warwick Montgomery wrote,

> In 56 AD Paul wrote that over 500 people had seen the risen Jesus and that most of them were still alive. It passes the bounds of credibility that the early Christians could have manufactured such a tale and then preached it among those who might easily have refuted it simply by producing the body of Jesus.[8]

In AD 67, as the apostle Peter's life was coming to a close and he was about to be executed, he wrote the following to all believers everywhere.

> *For we did not follow cunningly devised fables when we made known to you the power and coming of our Lord Jesus Christ, but were eyewitnesses of His majesty* (2 Peter 1:16).

Does that sound like a man who is about to be crucified for a lie? My paraphrase of what he was saying is, "Hey guys, I want you to know, we didn't make this stuff up. We're not lying. We actually saw Him raised from the dead in all His glory."

Around AD 90, the apostle John wrote,

> *That which was from the beginning, which we have heard, which we have seen with our eyes, which we have looked at and our hands have touched—this we proclaim concerning the Word of life. The life appeared; we have seen it and testify to it, and we proclaim to you the eternal life, which was with the Father and has appeared to us...His Son, Jesus Christ* (1 John 1:1-3 NIV).

It seems pretty obvious that these writers wanted us to know that they had actually encountered the resurrected Jesus, that this wasn't some fairytale they were making up. And they were willing to die to back it up. These three testimonies from Paul, Peter, and John have given me great assurance in my faith. They were simply telling their story to the world, and we know it was actually their story because the New Testament is a highly reliable source. Dr. Norman Geisler and Frank Turek wrote the following in their insightful book *I Don't Have Enough Faith to Be an Atheist*:

> We [have] powerful evidence that the New Testament documents were written by eyewitnesses and their contemporaries within 15 to 40 years of the death of Jesus. Add to that the confirmation from non-Christian sources and archaeology, and we know beyond a reasonable doubt that the New Testament is based on historical fact…The New Testament writers provoked their readers and prominent first-century enemies to check out what they said. If that's not enough to confirm their truthfulness, then their martyrdom should remove any doubt. These eyewitnesses endured persecution and death for the empirical claim that they had seen, heard, and touched the risen Jesus, yet they could have saved themselves by simply denying their testimony.[9]

The bottom line is that every one of the apostles died a martyr's death because they saw the resurrected Christ. The reason they were able to die that way is because the living Christ was inside of them, empowering them to be witnesses. The greatest news is that Jesus is just as alive today, empowering believers to both live and die for Him. One evening I was in prayer and said, "God, I wonder if I could ever die for You?" In response, His voice spoke gently to my heart, *"Just live for Me, son. When it's time to die, My peace will be with you."*

A MODERN ENCOUNTER WITH THE RISEN CHRIST

The resurrected Christ is still making appearances today, especially in third-world and Muslim countries. The next account is one that leaves little doubt that God is alive and still revealing Himself in supernatural ways. Bilquis Sheikh was a wealthy and devout Muslim woman in South Asia who had served Allah her whole life, but over the years she saw things within the Muslim world that disturbed her. One thing was the horrible abuse of women. In addition, Islam had left her empty and searching, but fearful. She had never read the Bible and knew nothing of Christ except what her Islamic teachers and the Quran had taught her—that Christ was a prophet and the Bible was a book of lies. But one day Bilquis witnessed the resurrected Christ firsthand, just as Peter and Paul did. Her story is truly miraculous in the way God got her attention during a period in her life when she was questioning her Islamic beliefs. One night, Bilquis had an incredible dream, or vision, that caught her by surprise. She said it was so life-like and real that when she woke the next day, she found it hard to think of it as a mere dream.

> I found myself having supper with a man I knew to be Jesus. He had come to visit me in my home and stayed for two days. He sat across the table from me and in peace and joy we ate dinner together. Suddenly, the dream changed. Now I was on a mountaintop with another man. He was clothed in a robe and shod with sandals. How was it that I mysteriously knew his name, too? John the Baptist. What a strange name. I found myself telling this John the Baptist about my recent visit with Jesus…"Where is He?" I said. "I must find Him! Perhaps you, John the Baptist, will lead me to Him?"

What followed after the dream was even more remarkable. When Bilquis woke up, she was calling out the name, "John the Baptist! John the Baptist!" She was yelling the name so loudly that two servants rushed into her room to comfort her. But here's the deal. Bilquis had never heard of John the Baptist! The name was completely foreign to her. Consumed with finding out who this man was, Bilquis knew of one couple she felt had the answer, but talking with them was strictly forbidden and dangerous. They were Christian missionaries, the Reverend and Mrs. David Mitchell. After considering the risks, she reluctantly snuck away to their home one night. After she arrived and was greeted by Mrs. Mitchell, the two women sat by an open fireplace. Mr. Mitchell was away on a trip to Afghanistan.

> "Would you like tea or coffee," she said.
>
> "Neither," I replied. "I have come to talk, not to drink tea...Mrs. Mitchell, please tell me, who is John the Baptist?"
>
> Mrs. Mitchell blinked at me and frowned. I felt she wanted to ask if I had really never heard of John the Baptist, but instead she settled back again in her chair. "Well...John the Baptist was a prophet, a forerunner of Jesus Christ...He was the one who pointed to Jesus and said: 'Look, the Lamb of God who takes away the sins of the world...'

After that, Mrs. Mitchell explained the Gospel and prayed for Bilquis, who was still not sure who this Jesus was. Mrs. Mitchell gave her a new Bible and instructed her to begin reading at the Gospel of John. When Bilquis got home, she did that. She soon read about John the Baptist, who pointed people to Jesus the Messiah. She recounted how in her dream she was asking John the Baptist where this Jesus was and how she was so desperate to find Him. Some time later in her bedroom, after crying out to Jesus, Bilquis had another encounter.

> Suddenly that room wasn't empty any more. He was there! I could sense His presence...For a long time I knelt there, sobbing quietly, floating in His love. I found

myself talking with Him, apologizing for not having known Him before. And again came His loving compassion, like a warm blanket settling around me…[10]

Bilquis Sheikh went on to serve Jesus and was used by Him to reach many Muslims. She suffered much persecution, which included her own family trying to kill her. But like the disciples who had seen the risen Christ, she too remained faithful. To read Bilquis' complete and utterly fascinating story, read her book, *I Dared To Call Him Father*. It's in the list of "Other Great Resources" in the back of the book.

There is no other way to explain what happened to Bilquis other than the Holy Spirit of God revealed the name John the Baptist to her in a dream to lead the way to Jesus and then Jesus/Holy Spirit showed up in her bedroom. He showed up for her, and He will show up for you and breathe His life into your dead situation, but in order to receive, you must diligently seek the truth. Hebrews 11:6 says, *"But without faith it is impossible to please Him, for he who comes to God must **believe** that He is, and that He is a rewarder of those who diligently seek Him."*

It all comes down to a choice. David Jeremiah said it well,

We have overwhelming evidence for the existence of God, the veracity of the Bible, and the historical life of Jesus on earth. Yet all this evidence leaves in our hearts a place that requires faith in order to come to full belief. The evidence will lead us on a long journey toward belief, but we will come to the place where the evidence points to a mystery into which we must plunge. Often people stop at the edge and insist on yet another piece of evidence as a stairway into the unknown. That is the point at which we must exercise the step of faith that forces us to trust in God and throw ourselves in.[11]

The evidence for the ***sanity*** *of belief* is available to everyone for evaluation and verification, but ultimately the choice comes down to you. Are you going to believe or continue in the ***Insanity*** *of Unbelief?*

> *I am the resurrection and the life. He who* ***believes*** *in Me, though he may die, he shall live. And whoever lives and* ***believes*** *in Me shall never die. Do you* ***believe*** *this?...* (John 11:25-26).

> *Most assuredly, I say to you, he who hears My word and* ***believes*** *in Him who sent Me has everlasting life, and shall not come into judgment, but has passed from death into life* (John 5:24).

> *For God so loved the world that He gave His only begotten Son, that whoever* ***believes*** *in Him should not perish but have everlasting life* (John 3:16).

> *He who* ***believes*** *in Him is not condemned; but he who does* ***not believe*** *is condemned already, because he has not believed in the name of the only begotten Son of God* (John 3:18).

> *Jesus answered and said to them, "This is the work of God, that you* ***believe*** *in Him whom He sent"* (John 6:29).

Lord, I believe; help my unbelief!
(Mark 9:24)

ENDNOTES

CHAPTER 1

1. Timothy Keller, *The Reason for God: Belief in an Age of Skepticism* (New York: Dutton, 2008), xvi.

CHAPTER 2

1. John F. Ashton, *On The Seventh Day* (Green Forest, AR: Master Books, 2002), 193.

2. *The Advocate*, Baton Rouge, LA (June 18, 2001), 6B. Emphasis is author's own.

3. Don Feder, "Why Hollywood Hates Christianity," *FrontPageMagaizne.com* (May 31, 2004).

4. H.S. Thayer, ed., *Newton's Philosophy of Nature* (New York: Hafner, 1953), 45.

5. Newton quoted in *Knight's Master Book of New Illustrations* (New York: William B. Eerdmans Publishing Company, 1956), 485.

6. Pierre Simon de LaPlace, *Evidences of Revelation*, 7.

7. Blaise Pascal, *Thoughts on Religion and Philosophy* (Edinburgh: Otto Schultze & Co, 1920), 5.

8. John Perry, *Unshakable Faith, Booker T. Washington & George Washington Carver* (Sisters, OR: Multnomah, 1999), 150.

9. Pierre Speziali, ed., *Albert Einstein-Michele Basso Correspondence*, 1903-1955 (Paris: Hermann, 1972), 425.

10. R. Clarck, *The Life and Times of Einstein* (New York: The World Publishing Co., 1971), 18-19.

11. Leo Tolstoy, *The Complete Works of Leo Tolstoy* (New York: Crowell, 1927), 378.

12. A.L. Rowse, *Shakespeare's Self-Portrait* (Lanham, MD: University Press of America, 1985), 182.

13. G.L. Geison, *The Private Science of Louis Pasteur* (Princeton: Princeton University Press, 1995), 141.

14. Arthur H. Compton, *Chicago Daily News* (Magazine Section, April 12 issue, 1936).

15. A. Cressy Morrison, *Man Does Not Stand Alone* (Westwood, NJ: Revell, 1944), 13.

16. John Ashton, *In Six Days* (Green Forest, AK: Master Books, 2000), 123.

17. Richard Swenson, *More Than Meets the Eye* (Colorado Springs: NavPress, 2000), 185.

18. Gerald Schroeder, *The Hidden Face of God* (New York: Simon & Schuster, 2001), 201.

19. Owen Gingerich, *God's Universe* (Boston: Belknap Press of Harvard University Press, First Edition, 2006), 120-121.

20. Phyllis Spivey, "Darwinism Discredited by Real Scientists," *In Plain Site;* www.inplainsite.org/html/scientists_discredit_evolution.html (accessed April 18, 2012).

21. H. Margenau and R.A. Varghese, eds. *Cosmos, Bios, Theos: Scientists Reflection on Science, God, and the Origins of the Universe, Life, and Homo Sapiens* (Open Court Pub. CO, La Salle, IL, 1992).

22. Stephen D. Unwin, *The Probability Of God* (New York: Crown Forum, Random House, Inc., 2003), 22.

23. John Ashton and Michael Westacott, *The Big Argument: Does God Exist?* (Green Forest, AR: Master Books, Inc., 2005), 51.

24. Ulrich Hildebrand. 1988. "Das Universum - Hinweis auf Gott?" in *Ethos* (die Zeitschrift für die ganze Familie), No. 10, Oktober.

25. Gabriel Meyer. 1996. "Pontifical Science Academy Banks on Stellar Cast." *National Catholic Register,* December 1-7 (North Haven, CT: Circle Media, Inc.).

26. F.J. Tipler, *The Physics of Immortality* (New York: Doubleday, 1994), preface.

27. George Greenstein, *The Symbiotic Universe* (New York: William Morrow, 1988), 27.

28. Robert Augros and George Stanciu, *The New Biology: Discovering the Wisdom in Nature* (Boston: New Science Library, Shambhala, 1987), 190-191.

29. George Wald, *Frontiers of Modern Biology on Theories of Origin of Life* (New York: Houghton Mifflin, 1972), 187.

CHAPTER 3

1. J.N. Willford, "Sizing up the Cosmos: An Astronomers Quest," *New York Times* (March 12, 1991), B9.

2. "What Life Means to Einstein: An Interview by George Sylvester Viereck," *The Saturday Evening Post* (October 26, 1929), 17.

3. George Wald, *Frontiers of Modern Biology on Theories of Origin of Life* (New York: Houghton Mifflin, 1972), 187.

4. Dean L. Overman, *A Case for the Existence of God* (New York: Rowman & Littlefield Publishers, Inc., 2009), 51.

5. Antony Flew, *There Is A God: How the World's Most Notorious Atheist Changed His Mind* (San Francisco: HarperOne, 2007), 133-145.

6. Stephen C. Meyer, "The Message in the Microcosm: DNA and the Death of Materialism," *Cosmic Pursuit* (Fall 1997), 41-42.

CHAPTER 4

1. Richard Dawkins, *The God Delusion* (New York: Houghton Mifflin Company, 2006), 113, 117.

2. Sam Harris, *The End of Faith: Religion, Terror, and the Future of Reason* (New York: W.W. Norton, 2005), 72.

3. C.S. Lewis, *A Grief Observed* (New York: Bantam Books, 1961), 4.

4. Fyodor Dostoevsky, *The Brothers Karamazov* (New York: Farrar, Straus and Giroux, 1990), 19.

5. *Medical Association Encyclopedia of Medicine,* Charles B. Clayman, ed. (New York: Random House, 1989), 658.

6. Roy Brunson, www.worldlightministries.org (accessed April 1, 2012).

7. Dr. Charles Stanley, podcast; www.learnoutloud. com/Podcast-Directory/Religion-and-Spirituality/ Christian-Living/InTouch-with-Charles-Stanley-Podcast/20116 (accessed April 19, 2012).

8. Christopher Hitchens, *Hitch-22, A Memoir* (New York: Twelve, Hachette Book Group, 2010), 340.

9. "Bruce VanNatta—Angels Among Us" television show on CMT, *Sweet Bread Ministries*; www.sweetbreadministries.com/scmedia.php? type=mediaplayer&loc=www.sweetbreadministries. com/media/media/mediaplayer.php&id=2011112910 1129C3D3ED&clientId=117565&client_id=117565 (accessed April 20, 2012).

10. Howard LeWine, http://health.msn.com/health-topics/articlepage.aspx?cp-documentid=100234835 (access April 20, 2012).

CHAPTER 5

1. C. S. Lewis, *The Screwtape Letters* (New York: HarperCollins Publishers, Harper Collins Edition, 2001).

2. Barna Group, "Most American Christians Do Not Believe That Satan or the Holy Spirit Exist" (April 10, 2009); www.barna.org/barna-update/article/12-faithspirituality/260-most-american-christians-do-not-believe-that-satan-or-the-holy-spirit-exist (accessed October 22, 2011).

3. Robert M. Price, *The Reason Driven Life: What Am I Here on Earth For?* (Amherst, New York: Prometheus Books, 2006), 253.

4. Dr. David Jeremiah, *I Never Thought I'd See The Day! Culture At The Crossroads* (New York: Faith Works, 2011), 48-49.

5. Chip Ingram, *The Invisible War: What Every Believer Needs to Know About Satan, Demons, and Spiritual Warfare* (Grand Rapids, MI: Baker Books, 2006), 45.

6. M. Scott Peck, M.D., *People of The Lie: The Hope for Healing Human Evil* (New York: Simon & Schuster, 1983), 182-184.

7. Chip Ingram, *The Invisible War*, 115.

8. James L. Garlow and Keith Wall, *Encountering Heaven and the Afterlife: True Stories from People Who Have Glimpsed the World Beyond* (Bloomington, MI: Bethany House, 2010), 106.

CHAPTER 6

1. Charles F. Stanley, "Listen to God, Walking with God," *In Touch Ministries*; www.intouch.org/resources/sermon-outlines/content/topic/listening_to_god_walking_with_god_sermon_outline (accessed April 20, 2012).

2. S. Mohr and P. Huguelet, "The Relationship between schizophrenia and religion and its implications for care," *Swiss Med Wkly* (2004) 134, 369-376.

3. Canonization is the process by which the Church eventually accepted certain Scriptures as divinely inspired and authoritative.

4. Charles Stanley, *How To Know God's Will* (Colorado Springs: NavPress, 1989), 12.

5. A.W. Tozer, *The Root of Righteousness: Tapping the Bedrock to True Spirituality* (Camp Hill, PA: Christian Publications, 1986), 21.

6. Corrie Ten Boom, *Not I, but Christ* (Grand Rapids, MI: Revell, 1997).

7. Anne Graham Lotz, *Pursuing More of Jesus* (Nashville: Thomas Nelson, 2009).

8. Randy Alcorn, "Is it possible to really hear God speak?" *Eternal Perspective Ministries;* www.epm.org/resources/2010/Mar/29/it-possible-really-hear-god-speak/ (accessed April 20, 2012).

9. Henry T. Blackaby and Claude V. King, *Experiencing God* (Nashville: Broadman & Holman, 1994), 136.

10. Rick Joyner, "Putting The AX to The ROOT of The TREE," *The Morning Star Prophetic Bulletin* (February 2008), 5-7.

11. Samuel Doctorian and Elizabeth Moll Stalcup, *God Will Not Fail You: A Life of Miracles in the Middle East and Beyond* (Washington DC: Believe Books, 2006).

12. Name has been changed.

13. Paul Yonggi Cho, *The Leap of Faith* (Gainsville, FL: Bridge-Logos Foundation, 1984), 40-44.

14. Henry T. Blackaby and Claude V. King, *Experiencing God: How to Live the Full Adventure of Knowing and Doing the Will of God* (Nashville: Broadman & Holman, 1994,) 132.

CHAPTER 7

1. Charles Colson, *Loving God* (Grand Rapids, MI: Zondervan, 1996), 55.

2. dc Talk and Voice of the Martyrs, *Jesus Freaks* (Tulsa, OK: Albury Publishing, 1999), 249.

3. "The Book That IS the 'Best Seller,'" *New York Times* (June 2, 1907).

4. Russell Ash, *The Top 10 of Everything* (New York: Dorling Kindersley Books, 1996), 112-113.

5. *British Times Newspaper* (1996).

6. Erwin W. Lutzer, *Seven Reaons Why You Can Trust the Bible* (Chicago: Moody Press, 1998), 51.

7. Mark Driscoll and Gerry Breshears, *Doctrine, What Christians Should Believe* (Wheaton, IL: Crossway, 2010), 63.

8. Norman L. Geisler and Frank Turek, *I Don't Have Enough Faith to Be an Atheist* (Wheaton, IL: Crossway Books, 2004), 225.

9. Ravi K. Zacharias, *Can Man Live Without God?* (Waco, TX: Word Publishing, 1994), 162.

10. Josh McDowell and Don Stewart, *Reasons Skeptics Should Consider Christianity* (Wheaton, IL: Tyndale House, 1981), 75.

11. Josh McDowell, *The New Evidence That Demands a Verdict* (Nashville: Nelson, 1999), 74.

12. W. Kenneth Connolly, *The Indestructible Book* (Grand Rapids, MI: Baker Books, 1996), 15-16.

13. Fredric Kenyon, *Our Bible and the Ancient Manuscripts*, 4th ed., rev. A.W. Adams (New York: Harper, 1958), 55.

14. Ibid., 23.

15. Dr. Nelson Glueck, *Rivers in the Desert* (New York, Grove, 1960), 31.

16. Jeffery L. Sheler, *Is The Bible True?* (San Francisco: HarperSanFrancisco, 1999), 59-61.

17. W. F. Albright, "Palestinian Inscriptions," *Ancient Near Eastern Texts*, edited by J. B. Pritchard, 3d ed. (Princeton: Princeton Univ. Press, 1969), 320-322.

18. "Sargon Brick Inscription," *Former Things;* http://formerthings.com/sargon.htm (accessed April 21, 2012).

19. Jeffery L. Sheler, *Is The Bible True?,* 99.

20. Ibid.

21. William G. Dever, "Philology, Theology, and Archaeology: What Kinds of History of Israel Do We Want, and What Is Possible?" *Archaeology of Israel: Constructing the Past, Interpreting the Present,* ed. Neil Asher Silberman and David Small (Sheffield, U.K.: Sheffield Academic Press, 1997), 20.

22. Ben Witherington III, "Top Ten New Testament Archaeological Finds of the Past 150 Years," *Christianity Today Online* (September 1, 2003); www.christianitytoday.com/ct/2003/septemberweb-only/9-22-21.0.html (accessed April 21, 2012).

23. N.S. Gill, "Pontius Pilate," *About.com: Ancient/Classical History;* http://ancienthistory.about.com/od/pontiuspilate/g/PontiusPilate.htm (accessed April 21, 2012).

24. Hilton Harrell Jr., "As Jesus said, 'Even the Rocks will Praise Him,'" Blog comments on Hershel Shenks, "Supporters of James Ossuary Inscription's Authenticity Vindicated," *Bar Magazine* (November 10, 2008); www.bib-arch.org/news/forgery-trial-news.asp (accessed April 21, 2012).

25. "Quotes From Some Scientists: Isaac Newton" *Valley Presbyterian Church and School*; www.valleypresbyterian.org/curriculum/science/quotes.htm (accessed April 21, 2012).

26. "How Life on Earth Began," *Reader's Digest* (November 1982), 116.

27. "Minerals Are Links Between Earth and Human Health," *Emory Report* (September 21, 1998) 51.5; www.emory.edu/EMORY_REPORT/erarchive/1998/September/erseptember.21/9_21_98Size.html (accessed April 21, 2012).

28. Arpad A. Vass, "Dust to Dust," *Scientific American* (2010) 303, 56-59.

29. Mitchell Waldrop, "Delving the Hole in Space," *Science* magazine (Nov. 27, 1981).

30. Matthew Fontaine Maury, *The Physical Geography of the Sea,* (New York: Harper, 1858), 250.

31. "Noah's Ark: Optimal Proportions," *World Wide Flood;* www.worldwideflood.com/ark/hull_form/hull_optimization.htm (accessed April 23, 2012). The team of nine research scientists were all on staff at Korea Research Institute of Ships and Ocean Engineering (KRISO) in Daejeon, Korea. Undertaken in 1992, the results were published in Korean the following year. The paper was translated to English and published in *Creation Ex Nihilo Technical Journal* (1994) 8.1, 26-35.

32. H.M. Morris, *The Biblical Basis for Modern Science* (Grand Rapids, MI: Baker, 1984), 295.

33. Grant R. Jeffrey, *The Signature of God* (Frontier Research, 1996), 107.

34. R.D. Ballard and J. F. Grassle, "Incredible World of Deep-sea Rifts," *National Geographic* (November 1979) 156.5, 680-705.

35. Susan West, "Smokers, Red Worms, and Deep Sea Plumbing," *Science News* (January 12, 1980) 117.2, 28-30.

36. Ibid.

37. Mark Hitchcock, *The Amazing Claims of Bible Prophecy* (Eugene: Harvest House, 2010), 8.

38. Hans-Wolf Rackl, *Archaeology Underwater,* Trans. Ronald J. Floyd (New York: Charles Scribner's Sons, 1968).

39. Merrill F. Unger, *Archaeology and the Old Testament* (Grand Rapids: Zondervan, 1954), 304.

40. Alfred Martin, *Isaiah: The Salvation of Jehovah* (Chicago: Moody Press, 1956), 76-77.

41. Quoted by S. Lewis Johnson, "The Word of God: The Ages Past"; www.sljinstitute.net/ (accessed April 23, 2012).

42. Matthew 2:1 of the Zondervan NIV Study Bible, 10th Anniversary Edition (1995).

43. Mark Hitchcock, *The Amazing Claims of Bible Prophecy* (Eugene, OR: Harvest House, 2010), 73.

44. Josh McDowell, *New Evidence that Demands a Verdict* (Nashville: Thomas Nelson, 1999), 193.

CHAPTER 8

1. Lee Strobel, *The Case for Faith* (Grand Rapids: Zondervan, 2000), 14.

2. "Epicurus," *Philosophy of Religion;* http://www.philosophyofreligion.info/whos-who/historic-figures/epicurus/#more-108 (accessed April 23, 2012).

3. N.T. Wright, *Evil And The Justice Of God* (Downers Grove, IL: InterVarsity Press, 2006), 73.

4. C.S. Lewis, *Mere Christianity* (New York: Simon & Schuster, 1980), 48-49.

5. Ibid., 52.

6. John Eldredge, *Epic* (Nashville: Nelson, 2004), 51-52.

7. Philip Yancey, *Disappointment with God* (Grand Rapids: Zondervan, 1988), 71.

8. Owen Gingerich, *God's Universe,* (Belknap Press of Harvard University Press; First Edition, 2006), 96.

CHAPTER 9

1. Nick Kalivoda, *Heaven's Password* (Radio Bible Course, 2000). Nick Kalivoda is founder of Radio Bible Course. He has a degree in Bible Archaeology from Wheaton College and a Master's in Journalism from LSU, and he studied at Dallas Theological Seminary.

2. A.W. Tozer, *The Pursuit of God: The Human Thirst for The Divine* (Camp Hill, PA: WingSpread Pulishers, 1982), 12.

3. Philip Yancey, *Rumours Of Another World* (Grand Rapids: Zondervan, 2003), 38-39.

4. Steven Waldman, "NPR Commentary by Steven Waldman September 4, 2003," *The Brights;* www.the-brights.net/vision/essays/waldman_futrell_geisert_npr.html (accessed April 24, 2011).

5. Dr. David Jeremiah, *I Never Thought I'd See The Day!* (New York: FaithWords, 2011), 25-26.

6. Information on these martyrs comes from: John Foxe, *The New Foxe's Book of Martyrs,* rewritten and updated by Harold J. Chadwick (New Brunswick, NJ: Bridge-Logos Publishers, 1997); dc Talk and Voice Of the Martyrs, *Jesus Freaks* (Tulsa, OK: Albury Publishing, 1999); Greg Laurie, *Why The Resurrection? A Personal Guide to Meeting the Resurrected Christ* (Wheaton, IL: Tyndale, 2004), 19-20.

7. Peter Kreeft and Ronald K. Tacelli, *Handbook of Christian Apologetics* (Downers Grove, IL: InterVarsity Press, 1994), 186.

8. John W. Montgomery, *History and Christianity* (Downers Grove, IL: InterVarsity Press, 1971), 147.

9. Norman L. Geisler and Frank Turek, *I Don't Have Enough Faith to Be an Atheist* (Wheaton IL: Crossway Books, 2004), 275, 300.

10. Bilquis Sheikh with Richard H. Schneider, *I Dared To Call Him Father* (Grand Rapids, MI: Chosen Books, 2003), 30-48.

11. Dr. David Jeremiah, *I Never Thought I'd See The Day!*, 32.

PEOPLE BEHIND THE STORIES

Marolyn Ford is a pastor's wife who is much in demand and is known internationally as an interdenominational inspirational author, speaker, and singer. For more information, go to her website, www.marolynford.com or contact Maroyln Ford directly through e-mail at maroylnford@bellsouth.net. You don't want to miss hearing her.

David Yaniv and his wife Sheila are pastors at Roots Messianic Congregation. There is also a docudrama about David's experience. To learn more about them, visit www.Rootsmessianic.org.

Bruce Van Natta now travels and ministers to churches and groups all over. Bruce's goal is to lead non-believers to Christ and believers into a deeper, more genuine relationship with Him. There are several videos of his encounter with angels and supernatural healing. For more information, see www.SweetBreadMinistries.com.

Captain Bob Bell has written a new book about his powerful experience titled *Between Life and Eternity*. To learn more, visit www.encounterpublishingllc.com.

OTHER GREAT RESOURCES

- *The Twilight of Atheism: the Rise and Fall of Disbelief in the Modern World* by Alister McGrath
- *I Don't Have Enough Faith to Be an Atheist* by Norman L. Geisler and Frank Turek
- *Reasons Skeptics Should Consider Christianity* by Josh McDowell
- *Beyond Belief to Convictions* by Josh McDowell
- *God's Universe* by Owen Gingerich
- *Is The Bible True?* by Jeffery L. Sheler
- *Zondervan Handbook To The Bible*
- *The Story of the Bible* by Larry Stone
- *The Bible Through the Ages,* by Reader's Digest
- *Unger's New Bible Dictionary* by Merrill Unger
- *The Indestructible Book* by Ken Connolly
- *Mere Christianity* by C.S. Lewis
- *I Dared To Call Him Father* by Bilquis Sheikh
- *Encountering Heaven and the Afterlife* by James L. Garlow and Keith Wall

- *Jesus: The Great Debate* by Grant R. Jeffrey
- *The Signature of God* by Grant R. Jeffrey
- *Letters From a Skeptic* by Dr. Gregory A. Boyd and Edward K. Boyd
- *Why I Believe* by D. James Kennedy
- *The Amazing Claims of Bible Prophecy* by Mark Hitchcock
- *The Case For Faith* by Lee Strobel
- *The Probability Of God* by Stephen D. Unwin, PhD
- *The Reason for God: Belief in an Age of Skepticism* by Timothy Keller
- *Defending Your Faith* by R. C. Sproul
- *Fingerprints of God: The Search for the Science of Spirituality* by Barbara Bradley Hagerty
- *Signature in the Cell: DNA and the Evidence for Intelligent Design* by Stephen C. Meyer
- *The Invisible War* by Chip Ingram
- *God Will Not Fail You: A Life of Miracles in the Middle East and Beyond* by Samuel Doctorian and Elizabeth Moll Stalcup, PhD
- *More Than Meets the Eye* by Richard A. Swenson, M.D.
- *Creation: Remarkable Evidence of God's Design* by Grant R. Jeffrey
- *The End of Reason* by Ravi Zacharias
- *Jesus Among Other Gods* by Ravi Zacharias
- *On The Seventh Day: Forty Scientists and Academics Explain Why They Believe in God* by John F. Ashton, PhD
- *In Six Days: Why Fifty Scientists Choose to Believe in Creation* by John F. Ashton, PhD
- *The Big Argument: Does God Exist? Twenty-four Scholars Explore How Science, Archaeology and Philosophy Haven't Disproved God* by John Ashton and Michael Westacott
- *The Hidden Face of God* by Gerald L. Schroeder

- *Saved by Angels* by Bruce Van Natta
- *Fearfully and Wonderfully Made* by Philip Yancey and Dr. Paul Brand
- *Where Is God When It Hurts* by Philip Yancey
- *The Jesus I Never Knew* by Philip Yancey
- *I Never Thought I'd See the Day* by David Jeremiah
- *What If Jesus Had Never Been Born* by D. James Kennedy and Jerry Newcomb

ABOUT MAX DAVIS

Max Davis holds degrees in Journalism and Theology. He's the author of over twenty books and has been featured on *The Today Show*, *The 700 Club*, and in the *USA Today* newspaper. Max is a dynamic speaker for both churches and conferences. Max and his wife, Alanna, live outside of Baton Rouge, Louisiana. To learn more visit www.MaxDavisBooks.com.